Photo: Chris Chapman

David Symes left Belfast University with an honours degree in microbiology in 1971. From 1980 he was freelance editing, concentrating on popular health subjects, and is now a publishing consultant on third world educational aid programmes. Along with the Family Heart Association he is also the author of the *FHA Low-Fat Diet Book*.

The Family Heart Association is a national charity helping the public, the medical profession and government to fight heart disease. Your help is needed to ensure that the work goes on:

- Support for patients with familial hyperlipidaemias or at high risk of coronary heart disease from other causes.
- Family information service for those wishing to adopt a diet and lifestyle with reduced coronary heart disease risk.
- Media information service.
- Information for the health professions, especially on blood lipid management and reduction of high coronary heart disease risk.
- Research on the early detection and prevention of coronary heart disease.

By David Symes and Annette Zakary, and published by
Optima as a companion volume to this book:

The FHA Low-Fat Diet Book

CHOLESTEROL
REDUCING YOUR RISK

David Symes
with the
Family Heart
Association

Illustrated by
Maggie Raynor

O P T I M A

An OPTIMA Book

First published in the United Kingdom
by Macdonald Optima in 1990

Published by Optima in 1993
This revised edition published by Optima in 1994

A CIP catalogue for this book
is available from the British Library

ISBN 0–356–21072–3

Typeset by Solidus (Bristol) Limited
Printed and bound in Great Britain by
Clays Ltd, St. Ives PLC

Optima
A Division of
Little, Brown and Company (UK)
Brettenham House
Lancaster Place
London WC2E 7EN

Contents

Preface to
second edition

Since this book was first written in 1990 there have been a number of developments in our knowledge of the links between blood cholesterol levels and coronary heart disease. For this new edition it was therefore decided to rewrite various sections of the book and to amend it heavily in other areas. It now reflects the most up to date thinking on:

- What we should all do to keep blood cholesterol levels within healthy limits and reduce our risk of coronary heart disease.
- What constitutes a high blood cholesterol level.
- What screening and monitoring should be available to detect raised blood cholesterol levels.
- What advice and treatment to offer people who have raised blood cholesterol levels.

David Symes
June 1994

Acknowledgments

As with any book such as this, a number of people have helped it along its way.

First of all, my very grateful thanks to Melissa Brooks, who was originally intended to write this book until a tragic family bereavement intervened. She did a lot of the initial spadework, and gave me very valuable help and encouragement when I was both researching the book and writing it. She was also responsible for editing the book, and has made a number of important amendments and improvements to it during this work.

The Family Heart Association provided considerable detail and suggested a number of important improvements. In particular, my thanks are due to Annette Zakary, BSc, SRD, at one time the dietitian/counsellor at the FHA, who has been tireless in her efforts to answer all my queries and odd questions. Specifically, Chapter 6, Practical help, has been pretty well entirely written by Annette. Much work for the second edition of this book was carried out by Linda Convery, BSc, SRD, the FHA dietitian, and by Dr Michael Turner, chief executive with the FHA.

Others who have given valuable help and asistance are: Dr John Betteridge, cardiologist, of University College Hospital; Mrs Linley Dodd, nutritionist, Perth, Western Australia; Mrs Linda Enos, occupational nurse, Wichita Falls, Texas; Dr A.D. Mehta, head of the Lipid Clinic at Torbay Hospital, Torquay; Dr Tim Dudgeon, GP at Moretonhampstead, Devon; Chas Mee, dispensing chemist, Chagford, Devon; Tom Sanders, BSc (Nutrition), PhD, King's College, London; Martin Perryman, farmer, Chagford; and Mrs W. Daymond, Chagford.

The diagram on page 91 is based on a similar chart in *Treat Obesity Seriously*, by John S. Garrow (Churchill Livingstone).

David Symes
January 1990

The publishers would like to thank Boehringer Mannheim, and University College and Middlesex School of Medicine for the photographs, and Maggie Raynor for the illustrations.

1

Introduction

Many people – perhaps most – when asked what the principal killer disease is in the UK would probably answer cancer. The public imagination seems to be morbidly fascinated with cancer, and with the media latching on to an ever wider range of cancers – lung cancer, bone marrow cancer, breast cancer, cervical cancer, skin cancer – there is an implicit belief that these cause more deaths than any other disease.

However, distressing though cancer is, it is not the chief killer in Britain. Nor are car accidents. Nor is AIDS. By far and away the leading cause of death in the UK is coronary heart disease – the clogging up of the arteries that leads to heart attacks.

If we look at the statistics in more detail, they make for grim reading. For example, in the early 1990s about 170,000 people a year died of heart attacks; that's nearly 500 people a day, or about one every $2\frac{1}{2}$ to 3 minutes. Within the UK population one in three men and one in four women will die as a result of coronary heart disease. It has been described, and rightly so, as a killer of epidemic proportions.

Within these bald statistics, two trends are worth noting. The first is that deaths from heart disease tend to increase as you go northwards in Britain; the south of England, the South-West and East Anglia have the lowest rates, while Scotland, Northern Ireland and the north of England have the worst rates. Indeed, Scotland and Northern Ireland have two of the worst rates for coronary heart disease in the world. The second trend to be noted is that deaths from coronary heart disease increase the lower down the ladder of social class you go, with those in unskilled work and the unemployed being three times as likely to die from coronary heart disease as those in the professional occupations.

How does the UK compare with other countries? Is this scourge of heart disease a global phenomenon? Yes and no. Coronary heart disease is a major killer in countries around the world, but not in all countries. With a few exceptions it strikes in those nations that have westernised cultures and lifestyles, particularly in the countries of northern and eastern Europe, north America and Australia and New Zealand. But all is not quite so gloomy as it might be. In the late 1960s it began to be realised that action could be taken to lower these rampaging death rates, and since then some countries have seen dramatic drops in deaths from heart disease, notably the US, Canada, Finland, Australia and New Zealand; for example, the US coronary heart disease death rates for men between their mid-30s and mid-70s fell by over 50 per cent in the period 1968–86.

These reductions in death rates were not chance events. They indicate that people were beginning to understand better the causes of coronary heart disease and were starting to act on this knowledge. For example, it was realised that the sedentary western lifestyle was a major problem – if you sat at a desk all day and took little or no exercise, you increased your chances of heart disease. People began to take more exercise and the jogging boom and the physical fitness crazes began. People also began to look at other areas of their lives, like smoking.

It also became apparent at this time that diet played a significant part in increasing the risk of coronary heart disease. A rich fatty diet tends to raise the levels of cholesterol in the bloodstream and, as our knowledge of the process surrounding the onset of coronary heart disease became ever more sophisticated, it was revealed that raised blood cholesterol levels in the population were a very strong predictor of subsequent heart disease. People therefore began to modify their diets, reducing their overall intake of fat, if possible substituting vegetable fat for animal fat, and eating more fruit and vegetables.

Has the UK benefited from this awareness of how to reduce the risks of coronary heart disease? Unfortunately not. While heart disease death rates dropped so dramatically in the US and other countries in the 1970s and 1980s, coronary heart disease mortality rates in Britain remained stubbornly high. Exercise and a low-fat cholesterol-lowering diet have been shown to lower the risks of heart disease, but this is a lesson that appears to have passed the British population by.

However, now these links are more clearly understood, it is to be expected that medical and public health education authorities will push them more and more into the public arena, and the connections between diet, blood cholesterol levels and coronary heart disease will become more and more a subject of general discussion. You will have heard a great deal

about cholesterol on TV and radio, and have read a
great deal more about it in the magazines and news-
papers.

What this book aims to do is to look specifically at
what cholesterol – this mystery substance – is, and
precisely what the links are between cholesterol, diet
and heart disease.

- The book tells you what cholesterol is.
- It tells you what coronary heart disease is.
- It explains who is likely to have high cholesterol
  levels.
- It details some policies that will help to bring down
  cholesterol levels nationally.
- It explains how the individual – you – can control
  cholesterol levels through your diet, and, just as
  important, it gives you a range of practical tips.
- It further explains how the risks of coronary heart
  disease can be diminished by changes to your
  lifestyle.
- It details over-the-counter and prescription remedies you can get for raised blood cholesterol levels.

The most important point to realise is that the book
shows you how you can take positive practical steps to
maintain a low cholesterol level or to lower a high
cholesterol level. In both instances you will reduce your
risk of suffering from coronary heart disease. Heart
disease is not unavoidable or incurable – it is within the
power of the individual to reduce their risks of suffering from heart disease and to reverse the symptoms.

One thread that runs right the way through the book
is that cholesterol itself is not a disease: the disease is
coronary heart disease, and it is a killer of epidemic
proportions in the UK and the other western countries.

Controlling our blood cholesterol level as part of a lifestyle overhaul is merely a means to an end, that end being the reduction of coronary heart disease.

Let us end this first chapter with a depressing but salutary tale.

John was an agricultural worker, so was used to taking plenty of exercise, particularly as the work was varied – the farm was a mix of cattle and sheep, so one seasonal job tended to run into another. Despite the long days and hard work he was mildly overweight, and ate a typical farmworker's diet – plenty of fried food, including a cooked breakfast every day, and regular sessions at the pub.

In his late 40s he began to realise that he was getting more breathless than he was used to feeling, but put this down to middle age. He certainly never thought of seeing his GP; the only times he ever saw him was when he needed stitching up as a result of some minor farmyard accident.

He then began to notice odd nagging pains in his chest after heavy physical exertion, but again didn't think too much about it. His wife tried to persuade him to see the doctor, but he pooh-poohed the idea.

A few days after his 50th birthday he was helping dip sheep – a heavy uncomfortable job, struggling with stubborn wet sheep – when he suddenly collapsed. The ambulance was there within 15 minutes, and the staff tried to resuscitate him on the way to the hospital, but he was dead on arrival.

The reason? A massive heart attack.

2

What is
cholesterol?

It you stopped a random selection of people in the street and asked them what they knew about cholesterol, you would probably get an ill-informed but revealing range of answers:

'Never heard of it, mate.'
'Is it to do with food?'
'I've heard of it, but can't remember what it's about.'
'It's something in fatty foods, I think.'
'It's bad for you, isn't it?'
'Isn't it something to do with heart disease?'
'It causes cancer.'

The majority of people would probably have heard of cholesterol, some would be able to link it with diet, some would even know of its links with heart disease, but the majority of answers would be very vague.

Perhaps the first step then, is to look at precisely what cholesterol, this mystery chemical, is and what it does.

WHAT DOES CHOLESTEROL LOOK LIKE?

Cholesterol is one of the most important animal lipids – naturally occurring fat-like substances. Chemically it is classified as a sterol, and has a complex chemical formula. If you obtained a solid block of cholesterol, you would see that it is white and waxy and quite soft at room temperature.

Much of the cholesterol in the human body is incorporated into complex structures, as we shall see later in this chapter. However, it can occur in a relatively simple and obvious form in circulating fat particles in the bloodstream; if the quantity of these cholesterol-rich fatty particles in the blood gets too much, cholesterol can be laid down in the lining of the arteries; and in individuals with very large amounts of circulating cholesterol in the blood, deposits of cholesterol and other fatty substances can appear in the skin, on the eyelids and at various other places around the body.

Chemical formula for cholesterol

WHAT DOES CHOLESTEROL DO?

Although the majority of people in the UK have only a vague idea of what constitutes a healthy diet, many are now aware that reducing the amount of fat we consume is a good thing, and some will tell you that high levels of cholesterol in the diet are a bad thing, and we would be far better off without it. However, this conclusion would be fallacious.

Cholesterol is, in fact, vitally important to the functioning of the animal kingdom; without cholesterol the human body would cease to work.

The cell membrane

The cell membrane is to the cell what our skin is to us; it keeps the insides in and the outside out. Unlike the skin, though, it allows the selective passage of some chemicals into the cell – oxygen and glucose, for example – and the passage of other chemicals, such as waste products, out.

To achieve these functions the cell membrane has evolved an extremely complex structure, despite the fact that it is microscopically thin. It is largely composed of proteins and lipids, and within the lipid element cholesterol plays a significant role.

The brain and nervous system

Most people have some idea of the brain being like a computer and the nervous system being like a telephone network linking the brain to the rest of the body. This implies that the brain and nervous system make use of tiny electrical messages and, as we all know, anything that conducts electricity has to be insulated from its surroundings. Similarly, the nerve pathways in the human body have an insulating sheath around them, and cholesterol is an important constituent of this sheath.

Vitamin D

Vitamin D is important in bone formation; it allows for the efficient uptake of calcium (the largest ingredient of bone) from the gut and ensures that it actually gets into the bones. Vitamin D is partly obtained from the diet, but is largely manufactured by the body as a result of sunlight reacting with fatty substances in the skin. And what are those fatty substances based on? Cholesterol.

Hormones

Here is not the place to go into the range and importance of the various hormones produced in the human body. However it is worth knowing that cholesterol is an important building block for both the sex hormones and the adrenal gland hormones, the latter being the steroid chemicals that we produce naturally.

Bile

Perhaps of most importance from the point of view of this book is that cholesterol is one of the chemical building blocks from which bile is formed.

Fats and oils will not dissolve in water or in a watery solution – the fact that oil and vinegar always separate out in a vinaigrette dressing illustrates this. We take in oils and fats in our food, and they somehow need to be mixed with the watery juices and food mass in our gut; if they are not well mixed in they cannot be digested and absorbed into the bloodstream.

Bile is produced in the liver – up to a litre a day, and looking like a rather disgusting car oil – concentrated in the gall-bladder, and then discharged into the gut when a fatty meal is eaten. Its job is to coat the fats and oils in the food and to assist in their dispersion into tiny globules and particles that can then be digested. Once the fats have been absorbed, the remaining bile passes on into the large intestine, and the bile salts – the constituents that contain the cholesterol – are broken down, absorbed and re-enter the production cycle.

These bile salts are important not only for the role they play in the digestion and absorption of fats and oils. Locked up in the fats and oils of our diet are essential fat-soluble vitamins such as vitamins A, D, E and K; without the presence of bile salts in the correct quantities we would run the risk of vitamin deficiency.

WHERE DOES CHOLESTEROL COME FROM?

So by now you will have realised that, far from being a villain that has no useful purpose in life, cholesterol is an absolutely essential part of our existence, although, as we will discover later, in excess it can be very damaging. But where does our cholesterol come from?

The majority of the cholesterol in the body is actually made in the liver and the small intestine, as much as 1 gram a day being synthesised at these sites. Even if we take in no dietary cholesterol, no dietary animal fat and only limited amounts of vegetable fat, as provided by a vegan diet, our body continues to churn out the cholesterol, with no attached risk and no detriment to our health and well-being.

However, if we consume what is known as a western

diet we take in a lot more fat than our body seems to be designed to cope with, particularly if we take little exercise.

- We take in **cholesterol** in our diet, largely from egg yolk, dairy produce and meat, particularly offal meat – liver, kidneys etc. The ingestion of dietary cholesterol should limit the amount of cholesterol made in the body, but the mechanism that controls this seems to work better in some people than others.
- We also take in large quantities of **saturated fats**, in the form of fatty meats and meat products, full fat dairy produce and processed vegetable fat, such as hard margarine; the higher the proportion of saturated fat in the diet, the greater the risk of excess levels of cholesterol circulating in the bloodstream.

Of the two factors, the proportion of saturated fat in the diet seems to be of greater importance in producing an excess of cholesterol in the system. However, as it tends to be the same dietary items that contain both saturated fats and cholesterol, reducing the proportion of saturated fat in the diet will automatically tend to reduce the amount of dietary cholesterol.

CIRCULATING CHOLESTEROL

We have established that cholesterol is a vital constituent of cell membranes, the nervous system, vitamin D, some hormones and the bile salts; that it is synthesised in the liver and small intestine; and that it can be derived from the diet. You won't need to be an expert in anatomy to realise that where it is needed and where it is made or absorbed are in different parts of

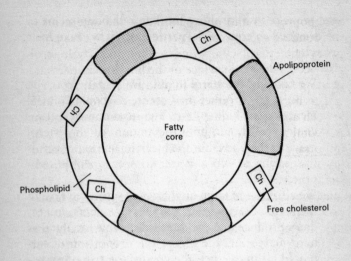

Diagrammatic cross-section of a typical lipoprotein

the body. So how is the cholesterol transported around the body?

The simple answer is in the bloodstream. But, like so many simple medical statements, this conceals a very complex picture that requires further explanation. It has already been shown that fats and water or watery solutions do not mix; the technical description for this is that they are immiscible. Cholesterol is a fat, and blood is a watery solution in which the blood cells are suspended. So what prevents the fatty cholesterol forming great greasy globules in the bloodstream and gumming the works up completely?

Basically it needs a water-soluble substance or a wetting agent, rather like a detergent, to ensure that the cholesterol stays in separate tiny particles and doesn't coalesce. These separate particles are called lipoproteins, and consist of water-soluble compounds called apolipoproteins and phospholipids – the detergents – surrounding a fatty core. Part of this fatty core comprises cholesterol compounds, while free cholesterol also occurs near the surface of the lipoprotein particle, nestling amongst the water soluble molecules.

This may seem a rather difficult concept to introduce at such an early stage; indeed, lipoprotein metabolism is a complex area of study, and is giving rise to a lot of important and exciting research. What is important to grasp is that cholesterol is transported in the bloodstream within tiny particles called lipoproteins.

However, understanding that cholesterol is transported in the bloodstream in lipoprotein particles is not the end of the story. Unfortunately, it's hardly the beginning of the story, for there are various different types of lipoprotein particle, with different amounts of cholesterol in them, with different functions in cholesterol metabolism and with different effects on our health. It is only possible to provide a very generalised overview of the whole highly complex mechanism, partly because of the restrictions of space and partly because it is not yet fully understood and much research is currently being carried out, providing new insights all the time.

Chylomicrons

Dietary fat is absorbed from the small intestine and combines with cholesterol, phospholipids and apolipoproteins (the wetting agents) to form particles called chylomicrons. Do not be put off by the name – chylomicrons are merely a form of lipoprotein.

As the chylomicrons pass around the body, they liberate fatty acids to the tissues – the muscles, for example; these fatty acids are either used as an energy source or, if not needed, are stored as fat. The remaining chylomicron particle, now rich in cholesterol, ends up being taken in by the liver and being processed.

Chylomicrons, then, are responsible for transporting cholesterol from the small intestine to the liver.

LDL

Cholesterol from the liver is passed into the bloodstream in a particle called a very low density lipoprotein or VLDL for short. Once in the bloodstream the VLDL 'matures', first to a particle called IDL (intermediate density lipoprotein) and then to LDL (low density lipoprotein). One key feature of this maturation from VLDL to LDL is that the lipoprotein particle becomes richer and richer in cholesterol; in fact the final LDL particle is the most cholesterol-rich lipoprotein in the bloodstream.

A large proportion of the LDL returns to the liver, where it provides the cholesterol for bile production. But the LDL is also taken up by cells in the peripheral tissues – muscle, skin, etc. – releasing free cholesterol into these cells. This release of cholesterol into the cells cuts back to the take-up of further cholesterol from the bloodstream and reduces the synthesis of cholesterol in the liver.

The important point to remember, though, is that LDL particles transport cholesterol from the liver to the peripheral tissues (including the arterial walls), and account for about three-quarters of the total circulating cholesterol in the bloodstream.

HDL

High density lipoprotein (HDL) appears to arise in the liver and wall of the small intestine, in a form known as nascent HDL. This nascent HDL 'matures' in the peripheral blood circulation, and during this process it gains cholesterol from the peripheral tissues. The blood

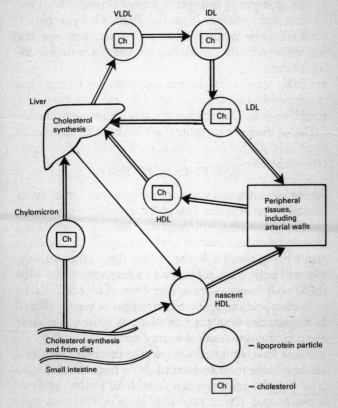

The relationship between the various lipoproteins as they transport cholesterol around the body in the bloodstream

circulation then transports the HDL to the liver.

The HDL lipoprotein particles thus appear to transport cholesterol from the peripheral tissues (including the arterial walls) to the liver.

Summary

- Cholesterol is transported around the body in the bloodstream, within particles called lipoproteins.
- LDL (low density lipoprotein) accounts for the majority of the circulating cholesterol in the bloodstream.
- LDL transports cholesterol from the liver to the peripheral tissues.
- HDL (high density lipoprotein) transports cholesterol from the peripheral tissues back to the liver.

MEASURING CHOLESTEROL

For various reasons your doctor – or you – may want to know what your blood cholesterol level is. To establish this you will probably have a small blood sample taken and sent to a laboratory for analysis, the result being sent back after a few days. Alternatively, you will have what is known as a fingerprick test – the tip of your finger is pricked, a drop of blood is placed on a chemical impregnated strip that in turn is placed in a machine about the size of a typewriter, and three minutes later the result is flashed up.

If you have a fingerprick test, the machine can give a reading of the total amount of cholesterol circulating in your bloodstream; it is not capable of giving the more sophisticated result provided by a laboratory. Furthermore, as with all laboratory equipment, these machines need careful calibration and quality control if they are to give accurate results. Therefore, if such a machine indicates that you have a raised blood cholesterol level, you should see your GP (if you are not already doing so) and ask for a more detailed laboratory analysis to make sure.

If you have a blood sample sent off to the laboratory for analysis you may be required to fast for a minimum of 12 hours before the blood sample is taken; the usual procedure is to take the sample in the morning, and ask you to have no breakfast, tea, coffee, etc., before coming in to have the sample taken. The reason for this has nothing directly to do with the blood cholesterol level, but concerns another group of lipids (fats) that are measured at the same time. This group, called the triglycerides, are very much affected by what you have eaten over the previous few hours, and an accurate and useful result can only be achieved after such food has been processed and metabolised by the body.

Total cholesterol

You may read or hear of blood cholesterol levels being referred to as total cholesterol, serum cholesterol or plasma cholesterol. These are all one and the same thing, and simply refer to the concentration of cholesterol in the bloodstream. This will be given in millimoles per litre (usually abbreviated to mmol/l), and in the UK the reading will probably be between 5 and 7.5 mmol/l, although figures both higher and lower than this do occur. To confuse matters, in the US they use a different system of units, called milligrams per decilitre (mg/dl); if you come across a blood cholesterol reading in mg/dl you need to divide by 39 to get a reading in mmol/l. i.e. 215 mg/dl is the same as 5.5 mmol/l.

The HDL:LDL ratio

If you have had a blood sample sent off to a laboratory your result may well come back with not only the total blood cholesterol figure, but also the breakdown of this figure into the LDL and HDL fractions. For example, you might have a total blood cholesterol of 6.0 mmol/l, with an HDL of 1.2 mmol/l and an LDL of 4.2 mmol/l. This gives a useful ratio, the HDL:LDL ratio, which is often discussed in conjunction with cholesterol levels.

You will remember that it is LDL that transports cholesterol from the liver to the peripheral tissues, including to the artery walls; there it can become involved in the furring-up process in the arteries that eventually leads to coronary heart disease. HDL, in contrast, transports cholesterol from the peripheral tissues back to the liver, and seems in some way to be able to remove some of the furring-up that leads to coronary heart disease; a raised HDL level certainly appears to give some protection against coronary heart disease. The HDL:LDL ratio is therefore valuable; if it is high it indicates the HDL level is high and the LDL level is low, which in very general terms is healthy; if the ratio is low it indicates that the HDL level is low and the LDL level is high, which in general terms is not healthy. (To confuse matters even further, in the US they often turn this ratio around, so it is an LDL:HDL ratio. This means that what has been said above needs to be reversed, i.e. a low figure is in general terms healthy, while a high figure is in general terms unhealthy.)

However, it must always be remembered that HDL, LDL and total cholesterol are all independent predictors of risk of coronary heart disease; combining these figures into a ratio like this can mask important information, so it is therefore essential that all three figures are examined separately and related to the individual and his or her lifestyle.

Triglycerides

The laboratory report will also give the fasting triglyceride level of the blood sample. This is of value, as a raised triglyceride level is a good predictor of a number of diseases; its relevance to coronary heart disease is not so clear at the moment though. But if both your cholesterol levels and your triglyceride level are raised your doctor will undoubtedly be extremely keen to get you on to a low-fat high-fibre diet in order to try and get both these figures reduced.

3

What is coronary heart disease?

As was pointed out in the introduction, the statistics relating to coronary heart disease are very alarming, particularly as so much heart disease is preventable. But what exactly is coronary heart disease and what is it caused by?

To begin at the beginning, all parts of the body need oxygen in order to function, just as a fire needs an air supply to burn. We take air into our lungs, and there it passes into the bloodstream and is transported around the body to where it is needed – muscles, brain, other organs and glands. All these organs and tissues also need nutrients – fuel – in order to function, and these nutrients are also transported around the body in the bloodstream. Waste products are removed from the tissues by the bloodstream and carried to the organs of excretion. Many of the functions of our immune system are carried out by constituents of the blood-stream circulating around the body. From this it should be clear that the bloodstream is an essential transport system, carrying a very wide range of products around the body.

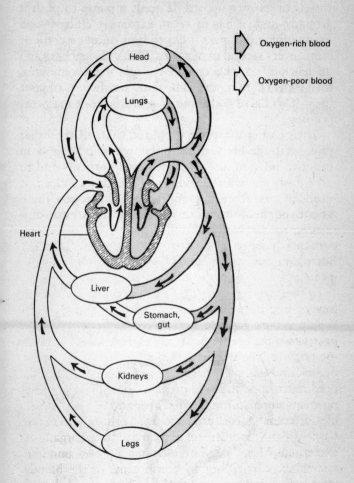

Oxygen-rich blood

Oxygen-poor blood

Head

Lungs

Heart

Liver

Stomach, gut

Kidneys

Legs

The blood circulation system

But the blood does not dribble around the blood vessels of its own accord. It needs a pump to push it around – and it has to be an extremely efficient and hardworking pump as it has to beat once a second or more, every second of our lives. Think of clenching and unclenching your hand every second for a few minutes, then think of doing the same thing for the rest of your life – it will give you some idea of the work the heart is doing.

The heart is a muscle itself and, like all the other muscles in the body, it needs its own blood supply in order to provide it with oxygen and nutrients and to take away the waste products it generates. Indeed, it needs a very efficient blood supply, when you think about the work it has to do during the course of a

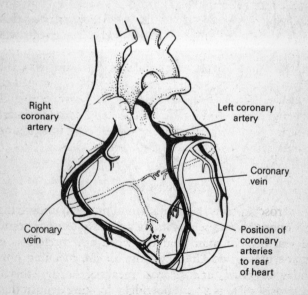

The coronary arteries serving the heart

lifetime. The blood vessels that supply the heart are the coronary arteries and veins, so called because as they loop around the heart they resemble a crown. The coronary arteries supply blood, oxygen and nutrients to the heart muscle, while the coronary veins take away the blood containing the waste products.

The coronary arteries are in fact the first arteries to branch off the aorta or main artery leaving the heart; this means that they carry the most oxygen-rich blood leaving the pumping chamber of the heart direct to the heart muscle. The larger coronary arteries are about the diameter of a large drinking-straw, but these soon subdivide to form smaller and smaller vessels that encircle and penetrate the blocks of heart muscle.

When you think of the regularity and constancy of the beating of the heart, you will realise that any damage to or disease of the coronary arteries that supply the heart muscle with oxygen and nutrients will have potentially disastrous results. If this essential fuel supply to the heart is compromised in any way the heart functions less and less well; blood is pumped to the rest of the body less efficiently; the heart complains when it is overworked. In short we have coronary heart disease – disease caused by the less efficient functioning of the coronary arteries of the heart.

ATHEROSCLEROSIS

Atherosclerosis is the fundamental problem underlying coronary heart disease, and is very easy to understand if you bear in mind that the word atherosclerosis is made up of two Greek words: *athere*, meaning porridge or gruel, and *scleros*, meaning hard. Atherosclerosis, then, is a hard porridgey-looking deposit that is found embedded in the walls of our arteries. The insides of blood vessels should be smooth and slippery to allow blood to pass through them as easily as possible; instead, atherosclerosis makes them rough and fibrous. Its effects are rather as you would expect if a domestic waterpipe were furred up – the blood supply is impeded and the heart has to work harder to pump the blood around.

The exact mechanism by which atherosclerosis builds up on the insides of arteries is not completely understood, but various processes are clear to see:

- There is initial injury to the lining of the blood vessel, allowing lipid penetration.
- Blood cells sensitised by LDL cholesterol work their way through the smooth lining of the artery.
- These cells that have invaded the artery wall take in more cholesterol-rich lipoproteins from the bloodstream, and thus form a so-called fatty streak in the artery wall.
- These processes further damage the lining of the artery, and other blood particles – platelets – adhere to the damaged areas forming scabs or clots.
- The blood particles in these scabs or clots release a hormone or chemical that encourages other cells in the artery wall to proliferate and invade the area, now known as plaque.

The result is that a cholesterol-rich scabby fibrous bulge appears in the artery wall, partially blocking off the artery and causing turbulence where there should be smooth efficient blood flow. The atherosclerosis can cause a weakness in the artery that may eventually rupture. In the worst cases the atherosclerotic area can effectively block the artery; alternatively, a bit of the

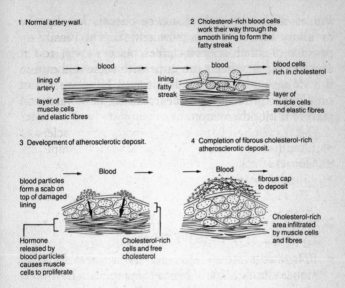

1 Normal artery wall.

2 Cholesterol-rich blood cells work their way through the smooth lining to form the fatty streak

blood

lining of artery

layer of muscle cells and elastic fibres

blood

lining fatty streak

blood cells rich in cholesterol

layer of muscle cells and elastic fibres

3 Development of atherosclerotic deposit.

4 Completion of fibrous cholesterol-rich atherosclerotic deposit.

Blood

blood particles form a scab on top of damaged lining

Hormone released by blood particles causes muscle cells to proliferate

Cholesterol-rich cells and free cholesterol

Blood

fibrous cap to deposit

Cholesterol-rich area infiltrated by muscle cells and fibres

The stages in the development of fibrous cholesterol-rich atherosclerotic deposits in the arteries

clot or scab that forms on top of the deposit can become detached and lodge across the artery some-where else, perhaps at another area of atherosclerosis, again blocking the artery.

Atherosclerosis can occur in the arteries in any part of the body, the resulting disease depending on the area of the body involved.

- In the brain it can cause a stroke.
- It can cause poor vision.
- It can cause kidney failure.
- If the legs are affected it can cause pain, lameness and even gangrene.

But it is the effect that atherosclerosis has on the coronary arteries that is most critical. The furring-up process of atherosclerosis takes place slowly, and it appears that the heart can cope with some diminution in its supply of oxygen and nutrients. However, it can only cope up to a point; beyond that point you will start to notice the symptoms of coronary heart disease:

- Angina.
- Heart attack.
- Sudden death.

Angina

Bob was a stores manager for a local building supplies firm. Most of his day was spent in the office, often on the phone. His only break during the day came at lunchtime, when he often went out for a hefty pub lunch with one of the reps from the building supplies companies. He was overweight, smoked a lot and was under a lot of stress at work, constantly trying to match supply and demand.

In his early 40s, he had been used to being breathless since his mid-30s, but had always assumed that this was due to his general lack of fitness. But then he began to notice a mild chest pain if he had to take any exercise out of the normal, run across the yard, for example.

One day he was involved in a ferocious argument with a delivery driver in the yard that left him almost immobilised with chest pain. After a few minutes sitting in his office it eased off, and he went to see his doctor the next day. His GP diagnosed angina, sent him for a thorough check-up at his local hospital, gave him advice on diet and exercise, and told him to stop smoking.

A year after the event Bob has done little to change his lifestyle and eating habits, is still breathless and overweight, and still gets attacks of angina.

Angina is a warning, a cry for help from the heart, that all is not well. It is an intense pain, often described as a gripping vice-like pain, originating in the chest; in many sufferers it spreads up into the neck and even down the left arm. It occurs at times when the heart has extra demands made of it, usually during bouts of exercise or hard work, or at times of stress. If you continue with the exercise or work the pain continues; however the pain is often so acute and distressing that the thought of doing anything other than keeping still is out of the question. After about 10 minutes of rest the pain disappears. The pain of angina may also be accompanied by breathlessness and shakiness.

What happens is that the coronary arteries that are partially blocked by atherosclerosis cannot get enough oxygen to the heart muscle to cope with the extra demands being placed on the heart. The result is that the acute pain of angina is felt, effectively stopping you from asking the heart to do something it is no longer capable of. So you stop exerting yourself, the heart's need for extra oxygen is gradually reduced and the pain goes away.

The effect of an angina attack is usually predictable. It frightens the person sufficiently for them to go and seek the advice of their GP, who, among other things, advises a low-fat diet, exercise, stopping smoking, etc. With luck and providing the person sticks to the advice and guidelines, the subsequent treatment should reverse the process of coronary heart disease and leave

them fit and well. The warning their heart gave had
been acted on.

However, if the person had ignored this warning, the
next stage is more dramatic – not so much a warning
as a punishment: a heart attack.

Heart attack

Linda is in her late 50s. She ran a mail-order firm
from home and was used to working long hours and
driving herself mercilessly. After the menopause she
began to put on weight and her health started to
deteriorate. At the same time her husband left her,
driven out, he said, by the pressure of Linda's work.

Linda had noticed some mild chest pains, particularly on busy days, but had not thought much
about them – they didn't inconvenience her that
much. Then one day, after a very hectic afternoon
getting stuff parcelled up in time for the post, she
was seized by an enormous gripping chest pain that
paralysed her, then left her grey, confused and
collapsed. She was rushed to hospital, to discover
she'd had a heart attack.

The process of recovery was long and slow, but
the story has a happy ending. Linda was able to sell
the business, although she still retains part-time
contact as an adviser. She's altered her food drastically to a low-fat, cholesterol-lowering diet, she's
taken up yoga and swimming, and has made contact
again with her husband. She's never felt better.

You may hear or read of a heart attack being described
medically under various terms. A myocardial infarction (MI) or acute myocardial infarction are commonly
used, both terms explaining very clearly what occurs:

infarction means the death of an area of tissue, and the myocardium is the heart muscle. So, myocardial infarction, or heart attack, means death of an area of the heart muscle.

If the blood supply to an era of the heart muscle becomes too impaired as a result of atherosclerosis, the area of muscle can start to degenerate. A sudden extra burden placed on the heart – work, exercise, excitement – can then be too much for it and that bit of muscle packs up. This is extremely painful, like angina but worse, and usually leaves you collapsed on the ground; it may even be fatal.

The severity of the attack will depend on the amount of heart muscle involved; if the damaged area is slight and there are no complications, the heart can function satisfactorily after a period of recovery, despite the fact that the heart attack has left it with a section of scar tissue instead of muscle. If the coronary heart disease is too far advanced by the time a heart attack strikes, the first attack may be fatal.

Sudden death

This is as dramatic as it sounds. Someone in apparent good health, and with no warning signs, drops to the ground and dies. A post-mortem invariably has to be carried out, and it is then the signs of coronary heart disease become obvious; the coronary arteries are usually furred up with atherosclerosis, to an extent that you wonder how the sufferer had survived as long as they had. Of course, this sort of event occurs in people with a history of coronary heart disease as well, but it is surprising how many people it affects who have no such history.

Eric was the finance director of a publishing firm. Once he had taken a lot of exercise – rugby, cricket, climbing, sailing – but pressures of work and family life had come to preclude any such leisure activities.

The family lived and ate well, very well by most standards, and Eric could usually reckon on an expensive business lunch two or three times a week at least. In his late 40s, and despite his office-bound lifestyle, he still looked fit and healthy, and certainly wasn't overweight. He smoked the occasional cigar, but had given up smoking cigarettes in his early 30s.

Coming home from work one day, he had to run from the underground to catch the train home from Paddington. He collapsed on the main station concourse with a heart attack, and was dead before the ambulance got there a few minutes later. Subsequent post-mortem examination showed that his coronary arteries were massively congested with atherosclerosis.

Unlike a heart attack, where part of the heart muscle is damaged due to lack of oxygen, in this case the lack of oxygen to the heart muscle involves so much of the heart that it loses any semblance of beating regularly in an organised manner, and goes mad. It is thus unable to circulate blood to any other part of the body, and death ensues rapidly.

CAUSES AND RISK FACTORS

Coronary heart disease is caused by atherosclerosis and compounded by thrombosis – clots. But what causes atherosclerosis? Unfortunately there is no simple answer. Even to say that there is a number of inter-related causes is a gross simplification. At the end of the day no one can tell you that if you do this or that you will definitely end up with coronary heart disease. True, our knowledge of cause and effect in the development of atherosclerosis and coronary heart disease is improving almost day by day, but there are still large areas of confusion where statements have to be hedged around with ifs and buts.

What we do have, though, is the statistical concept of a risk factor, i.e. if you smoke, you have an increased chance of coronary heart disease compared to someone who doesn't smoke. But be careful to note that this is not the same as saying that smoking causes heart disease. We all know of someone who smoked 40 cigarettes a day until they were run over by a bus at the age of 89; that they didn't die of heart disease (or lung cancer or any other of the diseases linked with smoking) much earlier in their life is because they were lucky enough to be among the small section of the smoking population who are predicted not to die of smoking-related illness.

So how is the concept of a risk factor arrived at. First, you obviously need an hypothesis, an idea, to test – for example that high blood cholesterol levels can increase your chance of coronary heart disease because the cholesterol is likely to become incorporated in the atherosclerotic matter furring up the arteries. To many this would seem a plausible idea. So you find two groups of people, one with high blood cholesterol levels and the other with low blood cholesterol levels, and you follow them over a period of years and count the number in each group who die of coronary heart disease. You might be encouraged to find that over, say, 10 years more people with high blood cholesterol levels died of coronary heart disease than did people with low blood cholesterol levels. Wonderful. This goes to show conclusively that high blood cholesterol is a risk factor for coronary heart disease.

Or does it? Perhaps the group with high blood cholesterol included a disproportionate number of smokers. Maybe the smoking caused the disease. Or did the smoking cause the high cholesterol? Or maybe the group with low cholesterol had a disproportionate number of women. Do women have a low risk of coronary heart disease, or do they have a naturally low cholesterol level? How much exercise did the members of the two groups take? By now you should begin to understand the complexity of establishing what the risk factors are and how serious is the risk attached to each factor. This is an area of much debate and controversy within the medical establishment.

However, within this controversy it is safe to list the following as risk factors for coronary heart disease:

- Raised blood cholesterol levels.
- High blood pressure.
- Smoking.
- Being overweight.
- Diabetes.
- Age, sex and ethnic origin.
- Genetic factors.

Of all the risk factors associated with coronary heart disease it appears that a raised blood cholesterol level is one of the most important, i.e. it is a strong predictor of risk. The latest research shows that if you reduce your blood cholesterol by 1 mmol/litre you will halve your risk of a heart attack.

Blood cholesterol levels

The process by which atherosclerosis builds up has already been discussed and from this it should be apparent why raised blood cholesterol levels are such a risk for coronary heart disease. As the atherosclerosis develops, cholesterol from the bloodstream is incorporated into its very structure, such that up to a third of the atherosclerotic deposit by weight is cholesterol. However, as we have seen in Chapter 2, the total blood cholesterol actually consists of a number of different cholesterol fractions, of which low density lipoprotein and high density lipoprotein are the most important.

- **Low density lipoprotein** transports cholesterol from the liver to the peripheral tissues. This includes transport of cholesterol to atherosclerotic deposits.
- **High density lipoprotein** transports cholesterol from the peripheral tissues, including atherosclerotic deposits, back to the liver, for eventual excretion.

From this it should be apparent that low density lipoprotein is the principal predictor of risk, as it is this LDL that helps to build up the atherosclerotic deposits that cause coronary heart disease. In contrast, high density lipoprotein actually reduces the risk of coronary heart disease as it removes cholesterol from the atherosclerotic deposits and transports it back to the liver so it can be broken down and excreted.

There is a danger of getting bogged down by the mass of figures when trying to establish what are 'good' and 'bad' levels for blood cholesterol. In brief, though:

- The total blood cholesterol level should be down towards 5 mmol/l, or even lower. If it is up towards 6.5 mmol/l you should seek advice on diet and lifestyle (and you should heed this advice); if it is up towards 7.5 mmol/l or above you should be very seriously advised on diet and lifestyle.
- LDL cholesterol should be as low as possible, preferably under 5 mmol/l.
- HDL cholesterol should be as high as possible, preferably over 1 mmol/l.

Blood pressure

High blood pressure, or hypertension, appears to increase the formation of atherosclerotic deposits in the arteries, and is thus a strong risk factor for coronary heart disease.

Blood pressure is merely a measurement of the pressure exerted by the heart as it pumps blood round the body. You will always see two blood pressure readings together, e.g. 120/70.

- The first is called the systolic pressure, and indicates the pressure exerted by the heart as it contracts and squeezes the blood out into the arteries. In the examples this is 120 mm Hg (short for millimetres of mercury, although the units need not concern us here).
- The second figure is called the diastolic pressure, and indicates the pressure when the heart is relaxed and is filling with blood. In the example this is 70 mm Hg.

It is difficult to establish hard and fast rules for what is a desirable blood pressure. The general rule is, the lower the better (although if it is too low it can cause other problems, like faintness on standing). Systolic pressure appears to be the better predictor of risk of coronary heart disease, and a systolic pressure below 140 mm Hg is advisable, with a diastolic pressure below 90 mm Hg; if it is over 160/95 mm Hg action certainly needs to be taken.

Smoking

The health risks of smoking are common knowledge these days and coronary heart disease is just one of those, very serious, risks. People who smoke more than 20 cigarettes a day have about double the risk of coronary heart disease as nonsmokers, and it takes about 3 years of nonsmoking for a reformed smoker's risk to drop to that of a permanent nonsmoker of similar age. Smoking is much more of a risk factor for coronary heart disease than being overweight, so if someone tells you that they don't want to stop smoking because they'll put on weight, you can point this out as the nonsense it is.

Being overweight

Many books on heart disease would head this section 'Obesity', which implies being extremely overweight. However being obese is not the same as being overweight; being overweight is merely being over a defined ideal weight for your height and sex. And various studies have demonstrated that there is a direct increase in risk of coronary heart disease with increase in weight above your ideal weight.

Diabetes

Atherosclerotic-related diseases are a serious risk for diabetics. Diabetics are two to three times more at risk of coronary heart disease, and are also susceptible to strokes, where part of the atherosclerotic deposit becomes detached and eventually lodges across a blood vessel in the brain, blocking it. Why diabetics should carry this increased risk is still not entirely clear. Women below the age of menopause have an inherent protection against coronary heart disease, but diabetes seems to remove some of this protection.

Age, sex and ethnic origin

The risk of coronary heart disease rises with age, from adolescence onwards. However, for women below the age of menopause this risk is always less than that for men; after the age of menopause women's risk of coronary heart disease starts to catch up with that of men, although it appears that at no time does it overtake it. The greatest difference between the risks for men and women is from the mid-40s to the mid-50s.

People from some ethnic backgrounds seem to have a fundamentally lower or higher risk of coronary heart disease; for example, people of Asian origin living in the UK have a greater risk than white people. This is not to be confused with risk of heart disease conferred by culture; for example, a Japanese living in Japan and eating a Japanese diet will have a low risk, but if he moves to the US and adopts a US diet and lifestyle his risk will rise to that of someone who has lived in the US all their life.

Genetic factors

It has been known for some time that coronary heart disease tends to run in certain families, but it is only with recent developments in molecular biology that we have been able to understand and categorise these problems. Perhaps the best known of these groups of problems are the inherited familial hyperlipidaemias; hyperlipidaemia means very high levels of blood lipids, such as cholesterol, and in these cases they are caused by an inherited defect in lipid metabolism. Different inherited defects cause different lipoprotein levels to be raised, but the end result is the same – very high risk of coronary heart disease, with heart attacks often occurring before the age of 40 or even 30 in men who are affected.

For more information on familial hyperlipidaemias, and on coronary heart disease prevention, consult the Family Heart Association.

4

Detecting those at risk

Assessing the risk of coronary heart disease in an individual is not quite as easy as it sounds. You can probably safely assume that a slim fit woman who takes plenty of exercise, is of childbearing years, who doesn't smoke and who comes from a family with no history of heart problems is unlikely to have a heart attack tomorrow. At the other end of the spectrum is the overweight 50-year-old man who sits at his desk all day, smokes a lot, copes badly with stress and eats a fatty diet. However the majority of people fall somewhere in between, with different levels of risk for different factors.

As has already been observed, one of the most important of these risk factors is the level of cholesterol circulating in the blood. If this is raised, then the risk of coronary heart disease is also raised; for every 1 per cent the cholesterol level is raised, the risk of coronary heart disease is raised by 2 per cent. Fortunately the converse is equally true. If it is possible to identify and treat those people who have raised cholesterol levels, there is a good chance of reducing their risks of suffering from coronary heart disease.

In this chapter we will therefore be looking at how those individuals most at risk can be detected.

WHO HAS HYPERLIPIDAEMIA?

Hyper comes from a Greek word meaning over or beyond; in medical terms it means raised, as in hypersensitive, excessively sensitive, or hypertension, raised blood pressure. Hyperlipidaemia therefore means raised level of lipids circulating in the blood system, i.e. raised levels of cholesterol and, to a lesser extent, triglycerides in the blood.

So, who does have hyperlipidaemia, or raised blood cholesterol levels? It is important to have this information, as it may well be possible to bring their blood cholesterol levels down, and in this way lessen the risk of coronary heart disease. Many people will in fact have what are called secondary hyperlipidaemias, i.e. the raised blood cholesterol levels are a result of – are secondary to – another problem. If the other problem can be solved, the raised blood cholesterol levels should return to normal. The principal reasons for these secondary hyperlipidaemias are:

- Diet and lifestyle.
- Side effects of drugs.
- Side effects of illnesses.

High blood cholesterol levels caused by these problems can invariably be sorted out. However there is another reason why someone may have hyperlipidaemia, and that is because of a fundamental inherited fault in their body chemistry. These familial hyperlipidaemias pose a much more intractable problem, simply because the underlying problem cannot be cured.

Diet and lifestyle

The ever-increasing advance of affluence in what are described as the western cultures or western economies has brought us benefits that our forebears would never have dreamed of, even as recently as a hundred years ago. However, hand in hand with these benefits have emerged problems: medicine has diminished the threat of the infectious diseases and has lengthened our lifespan, but we now have what might be described as the diseases of longevity; we have all sorts of aids to daily living, but take less exercise as a result; we can pack a lot more into our day, but the toll that stress takes becomes ever more apparent; we can afford and can obtain a very rich and varied diet, but this often seems to overload our systems. These are all generalisations, applying across the western world as a whole. But one specific statement can be made with certainty; the western diet and lifestyle that we all take for granted and, presumably, enjoy so much is the principal reason why people have high cholesterol levels in their blood and, as a result, why so many people in the west suffer from and die of coronary heart disease. If the western peoples were overnight to reduce their consumption of fat, and particularly of saturated fat, and to take more exercise, blood cholesterol levels would rapidly start to fall and the incidence of coronary heart disease would similarly drop.

Interestingly, Europe has been through such an experience relatively recently. Between 1939 and 1950 Europe was first plunged into the turmoil of a war that spread across the whole continent, and then had to suffer the chaos, confusion and diminished supplies that were a consequence of it. Everything that we take for granted now – ample food, transport, leisure time – was rationed or was simply not there. In short, the fruits of our western economy were removed, for some countries at a stroke. For example, in the UK during the 1940s, a typical adult could expect to receive:

- Butter – 2 ounces a week.
- Margarine – 4 ounces a week.
- Eggs – two a week, plus dried egg when it was available.
- Cheese – 2 ounces a week, except agricultural workers, who were allowed 8 ounces a week.
- Sugar – very limited.
- Meat and bacon – certainly not enough to allow a meat or bacon based meal every day.

There were many consequences of this enforced change of diet and lifestyle, but one particular consequence should be of great interest to us; atheroscelerotic deposits in the arteries, as noted during post-mortems and autopsies, became much harder to find than they had been before the war. As the standard of living gradually began to rise after the war, as rationing was reduced and food supplies became more plentiful and more varied, so the reports of atherosclerosis began to increase again.

The links between diet, atherosclerosis and coronary heart disease were not nearly so well understood then as they are now, so at the time it was not possible to draw the conclusions we can draw today. But it does seem that the limited diet that was available, with a very significant reduction in meat and dairy produce, coupled with an increase in exercise because of a general shortage of transport, lowered cholesterol levels across the population as a whole, with a concomitant and noticeable reduction in atherosclerosis.

In recent years the study of diet, blood lipid levels and the incidence of coronary heart disease has become a major area of medical research, such that we can now be much more specific about what aspects of our diet are responsible for high cholesterol levels and, as a result, the high rates of coronary heart disease. A more detailed examination of diet and cholesterol levels will be found in Chapter 5; at this point it is merely necessary to state that all of us in the west eat too much fat. Meat and meat products contain high levels of fat; milk contains a relatively significant proportion of fat; cheese and other dairy produce contain a high proportion of fat; pastries, biscuits and cakes contain a high proportion of fat; fried foods contain a high proportion of fat. This is not to say that these foods are inherently dangerous; merely that if your diet largely consists of these foods you will, perhaps unwittingly, consume more fat than your body can cope with and as a result it is extremely likely that you will have a high cholesterol level. The hyperlipidaemia is thus secondary to the diet; change the diet – lower the intake of fats, particularly saturated fats, and increase the intake of non-fatty foods, particularly complex carbohydrates, fruit and vegetables – and the cholesterol level will come down.

There are other aspects of our western lifestyle that contribute to this problem. In general, we don't take enough exercise, and certainly don't take enough strenuous exercise; the more exercise we take, the more we are likely to lower our blood lipid levels. Specifically, exercise appears to lower the level of LDL cholesterol in the blood, the lipoprotein that transports cholesterol to peripheral tissues, and furred-up arteries, and to raise the level of HDL cholesterol in the blood, the lipoprotein that transports cholesterol away from the peripheral tissues and the furred-up arteries.

In summary, then, it is fair to say that most people who have hyperlipidaemia, including raised blood cholesterol levels, will be suffering from this problem because of their diet and lifestyle.

Side effects of drugs

Doctors today have an enormous battery of drugs which they can use to treat every conceivable disease and disorder. All these prescribed drugs are rigorously tested before their use is sanctioned. However drugs do have side effects; some are known when their use is sanctioned; other side effects become apparent after long-term use. Some of the side effects are deemed harmless, others might be deemed to have a slight risk attached but much less than the risk attached to the disease the drug treats. Occasionally a side effect that was initially thought harmless is discovered, in fact, to have a risk attached to it.

There are some prescribed drugs that can cause an elevation of blood lipid levels, i.e. the hyperlipidaemia is secondary to the use of the prescribed drug. Ironically, two groups of drugs that have been particularly shown to raise blood lipid levels are used to treat another aspect of heart disease, hypertension, or high blood pressure. Thiazide diuretics and, of more significance, beta-blockers are both used to treat high blood pressure, while beta-blockers are also used to treat other heart problems such an angina. Both groups of drugs can cause raised blood lipid levels, although within each group some of the drugs have considerably less effect on the circulating lipid levels than others.

Use of some steroid drugs can raise blood lipid levels, and long-term use of some oral contraceptives, for example, over 10 years, has been known to cause problems with raised blood lipid levels.

Side effects of illnesses

A number of illnesses can have a direct and often dramatic effect on the body's lipid metabolism, causing a markedly raised blood cholesterol. If the underlying disease can be dealt with or controlled, the cholesterol levels can be brought down to reasonable levels and the risk of coronary heart disease thus diminished.

Diabetes is perhaps the most well-known disease that causes such problems. Diabetes can be divided into two forms. There is insulin-dependent diabetes mellitus (IDDM) or type I diabetes, in which the body fails to produce the hormone insulin and the body's metabolism of glucose is thrown awry. The other form is non-insulin-dependent diabetes mellitus (NIDDM) or type II diabetes, affecting older people, in which the insulin doesn't function properly. Both types of diabetes can produce raised blood lipid levels, but NIDDM in particular can produce raised blood cholesterol levels.

IDDM diabetes is usually treated with injections of insulin, while NIDDM diabetes is usually treated by changing to a high-fibre, low-fat, low-refined-sugar diet and by weight reduction – most NIDDM diabetics are overweight. The treatment for NIDDM diabetics might sound a little familiar. Being overweight is a significant risk factor in heart disease, and earlier in this chapter you will have learned that a rich fatty diet with little in the way of fruit and vegetables produces raised cholesterol levels. It will therefore be apparent that a NIDDM diabetic has to keep as much of an eye on his or her blood lipid levels as they do on their blood glucose levels, the corollary being that a diet that is good for one tends to be good for the other as well.

The thyroid gland is situated in the neck and produces a hormone called thyroxine. Thyroxine has a number of roles within the body, one of which has an effect of lipid metabolism; put simply, if there is a shortage of this hormone blood lipid levels, and particularly the level of low density lipoprotein, rise. This is called hypothyroidism (from the Greek word *hypo* meaning shortage of), and is invariably treated by taking thyroid hormone pills; once treatment has begun the elevated cholesterol levels usually fall rapidly, if this is the problem.

Diseases of the liver and kidneys can also cause raised blood cholesterol levels, but they are not so common. Alcohol use can also raise cholesterol levels, although triglyceride levels are more usually elevated.

What all this means is that, if it is discovered that you have a raised blood cholesterol level, your doctor will first of all make certain that is not caused by any underlying disease that has not been spotted. At the same time you will (or should) be advised on diet and exercise and other aspects of your lifestyle. But if you are discovered to have a seriously raised blood cholesterol level, and particularly if other members of your family have suffered from coronary heart disease early in their lives, your doctor will begin to look out for the telltale signs of a fundamental inherited problem in lipid metabolism.

PRIMARY HYPERLIPIDAEMIA

We have already come across the word hyperlipidaemia – it means raised lipid levels in the blood, and as far as this book is concerned we are considering raised cholesterol levels. And we have examined the term secondary hyperlipidaemia, where the raised blood cholesterol level is caused by, or is secondary to, some other problem, e.g. prescribed drugs, illness. But what is primary hyperlipidaemia?

Primary hyperlipidaemia again means that we are looking at raised blood cholesterol levels. However, unlike secondary hyperlipidaemia, here the problem is the disorder and the disorder is the problem; the problem is a disorder in lipid metabolism – the manner in which the body processes fats at a molecular level – and this manifests itself as high (often extremely high) blood cholesterol levels, which in turn give a very high risk of coronary heart disease.

When I was 22 years of age I returned home from doing two years National Service in the Royal Air Force. My mother, who was 54 years old, then suddenly had a heart attack and died. In those days the cause of death was recorded as 'hardening of the arteries'. I remember our family doctor simply saying that this sometimes happened as people got older, and little seemed to be known about the causes, and no advice was given to other members of the family.

The next 25 years passed uneventfully, with myself and my two other brothers getting married and bringing up our own families, but as I reached middle age I noticed that I was getting breathless and sometimes had severe pains at the top of my back. It was only after several visits to the doctor over four or five years that it was suggested that I should have a blood test, which revealed that I had a cholesterol level of 14.7. In the meantime my elder brother, who was five years older than myself, died from a heart attack. It now appears that my grandfather, who died at 42 years of age, my mother, and my brother who died at 57 all had the inherited condition known as familial hypercholesterolaemia (FH). This is the same condition that I was diagnosed as having when I attended the hospital lipid clinic. Further examination showed that I had severe narrowing of the coronary arteries, and a coronary bypass operation was recommended.

It was at this point that I made one of the biggest decisions of my life, and after four or five tormented days, I decided to tell the specialist that I was not prepared to have the operation, and asked if there was any other form of treatment that he could recommend. Fortunately, he didn't tell me to get lost, and said that if I was absolutely adamant about this, he could include me in a small group of people who would undergo a fortnightly blood-filtering process known as apheresis. This would remove the LDL from the blood whilst leaving a higher concentrate of HDL, in the hope that it would remove the deposits from the arterial wall. After 18 months' treatment, plus cholesterol-lowering drugs and a healthy fat-free diet, periodical exercise ECGs showed that my condition was gradually improving. Then a further angiograph showed that many of the smaller arteries had opened up, and my breathlessness and pains are now non-existent. My present cholesterol level is 6.2, which for me is very good.

As a result of my finding out that I had FH, my other brother was tested and is now on treatment, and my one son has also been tested and it appears that he has not inherited the condition. I feel that had I known that my cholesterol level was dangerously high early enough in life, and been able to take steps to reduce it, it could have saved me a considerable amount of discomfort and the very real possibility of having a heart attack.

The metabolic disorders underlying these diseases are beyond the scope of this book. What is important to know is that they are all inherited, i.e. if one person in the family is discovered to be suffering from a primary hyperlipidaemia, then other members of the family are also likely to be suffering from the same problem, and this problem will be passed down from generation to generation. Indeed, these are amongst some of the commonest inherited disorders, with perhaps as many as one in 300 persons suffering from what is known as familial combined hyperlipidaemia, and, in the UK, about one person in 500 suffering from familial hyper-cholesterolaemia (amongst Afrikaners and Lebanese and incidence is even higher). The inheritance of the other primary hyperlipidaemias is not so well under-stood and their prevalence amongst the population at large not so well known.

The majority of the primary hyperlipidaemias cause raised cholesterol levels, usually with raised triglyceride levels as well. For an average adult a blood cholesterol level of 7.5 mmol/l would usually be considered unac-ceptably high; for someone suffering from an untreated form of primary hyperlipidaemia this would be low and might be virtually unobtainable. Levels of 8–12 mmol/l would be routine in untreated patients, and in the case of familial hypercholesterolaemia (mercifully, usually abbreviated to FH) levels well above 12 mmol/l are not uncommon.

This means that such individuals are at great risk of coronary heart disease. For example, men suffering

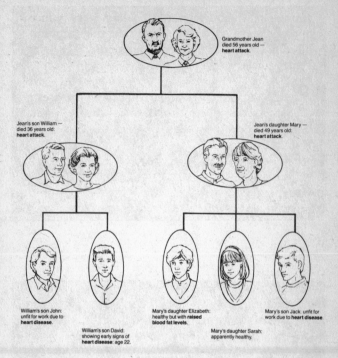

Grandmother Jean died 56 years old — **heart attack**.

Jean's son William — died 36 years old: **heart attack**.

Jean's daughter Mary — died 49 years old: **heart attack**.

William's son John: unfit for work due to **heart disease**.

William's son David: showing early signs of **heart disease**: age 22.

Mary's daughter Elizabeth: healthy but with **raised blood fat levels**.

Mary's daughter Sarah: apparently healthy.

Mary's son Jack: unfit for work due to **heart disease**.

A typical family with hypercholesterolaemia (FH)

from FH have an eight-fold greater chance of suffering from coronary heart disease compared to unaffected men. Coronary heart disease thus tends to strike at a much earlier age than in the unaffected public; the very high levels of cholesterol circulating in the bloodstream are able to fur-up the arteries much more rapidly. Sometimes the results can be extremely distressing: young men in their 30s, or even in their 20s, completely incapacitated by coronary heart disease; men struck down by fatal heart attacks when they should be in the prime of their lives.

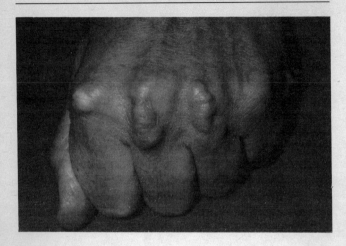

(a)

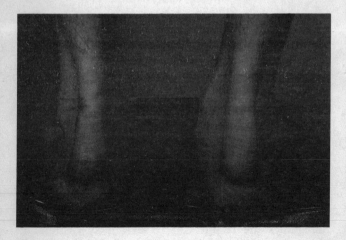

(b)

Tendon xanthomata on the knuckles (a), the ankles (b) and the knees indicate high blood cholesterol levels

As the primary hyperlipidaemias involve such high levels of circulating cholesterol, the cholesterol tends to be deposited at various sites around the body, depending on precisely which hyperlipidaemia is involved. These deposits then show up on examination, and doctors should routinely keep an eye open for such signs, which are easy to understand and often easy to spot:

- Tendon xanthomas.
- Corneal arcus.
- Xanthomas on elbows.
- Palmar xanthomas.
- Xanthelasmas.

Tendon xanthomas

The tendons are the stringy bits the join the muscles to the bones; you find them in particular around the joints of the body. And a xanthoma is a yellow deposit, from *xanthos* the Greek word meaning yellow.

Tendon xanthomas, then, are yellowish deposits seen as bulges or lumps in what are normally rather scrawny parts of the body. These bulges or lumps consist largely of cholesterol, and are seen either on the Achilles tendon above the heel or the tendons just above the knuckles on the back of the hand. These xanthomas are particularly common in people suffering from FH.

Corneal arcus

This is a whitish or yellowish ring around the outside of the iris (the coloured part of the eye), and consists of cholesterol deposits within the iris. Again, it is associated with FH, but can also be found in two other primary hyperlipidaemias, common hypercholester-olaemia and familial combined hyperlipidaemia (FCH).

Xanthomas on elbows

These are knobbly yellow or white lumps under the skin of the elbow. Larger deposits are referred to as tuberous xanthomas and are typical of something called remnant hyperlipidaemia; smaller deposits, called eruptive xanthomas, may also be found on the buttocks, and are typical of familial hypertriglycer-idaemia and chylomicronaemia syndrome.

Palmar xanthomas

These are yellowish-white cholesterol deposits found under the skin in the creases of the palms of the hands.

Corneal arcus – the whitish ring around the iris of the eye – is an early sign of raised blood cholesterol levels

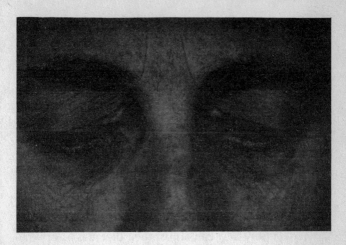

Xanthelasmus on the eyelids are another sign of raised blood cholesterol levels

They are a typical sign of remnant hyperlipidaemia; this is a less common form of primary hyperlipidaemia than FH, but is an equally serious cause of coronary heart disease of early onset.

Xanthelasmas

Finally there are xanthelasmas, small fatty blobs that develop around the eye or eyelid. Sometimes these get large enough to resemble droopy warts. They are found typically in people who suffer from common hyper-cholesterolaemia, FH and FCH.

DETECTION OF RAISED CHOLESTEROL LEVELS

The pertinent question, then, is what sort of people are likely to have raised blood cholesterol levels?

Coronary heart disease

It may seem like stating the obvious, but those people who have suffered from coronary heart disease already are extremely likely to have high blood cholesterol levels; if they have not got their circulating cholesterol levels down to healthy limits they are putting themselves at great risk of allowing the heart disease to take a further toll on their health and life.

You might expect that anyone who has suffered from heart disease – angina or a previous heart attack – or who has undergone surgery to relieve coronary heart disease symptoms, would regularly have their blood cholesterol levels checked and would be given very firm advice on how they can adjust their diet and lifestyle to keep their cholesterol levels as low as possible. There is an extremely good chance that their coronary heart disease was initially linked to, among other things, high circulating cholesterol levels; treating the symptoms of heart disease without treating one of the causes undermines any chances of controlling or eliminating the disease.

It should therefore be of prime importance that anyone who has a history of coronary heart disease should have their blood cholesterol levels checked regularly.

Heart disease in relatives

We have already looked at the problem of hyper-lipidaemias (pages 30–5), where an abnormally high blood cholesterol level is caused by an inherited defect in lipid metabolism. Such a high cholesterol level then gives a much greater risk of coronary heart disease, often at what might be considered an early or premature age – certainly before the age of 55, and often in the 40s or 30s.

But what happens if we turn these statements round? Someone suffers from coronary heart disease in their 40s, let's assume. This is a premature age for heart disease, taking the population as a whole, and there may be a chance that the underlying cause of this early coronary heart disease is one of these primary hyperlipidaemias. We know that the primary hyperlipidaemias are inherited. We must therefore draw the conclusion that there may be other people in the same family – not just brothers, sisters and children, but also cousins, nephews, nieces, uncles, aunts, etc. – who are in the same predicament. If this is the case, and the family as a whole has an inherited primary hyperlipidaemia running through it, some members of the family may already have started to suffer from symptoms of heart disease, while some of the older members may have already died of heart disease. Other members will have raised blood cholesterol levels but the symptoms of coronary heart disease may not have become apparent.

If, therefore, there appears to be a strong family history of heart disease, all members of the family should have their blood cholesterol levels checked. If someone starts to develop symptoms of heart disease at a premature age, i.e. before the age of 55, the other members of the family should be checked as a matter of course. And if someone is diagnosed as having one of the primary hyperlipidaemias, particularly FH or FCH, all the other members of the family should be checked as a matter of some urgency. In this way if there are any members of the family who have high cholesterol levels, but who have not yet developed symptoms of coronary heart disease, they can be identified and

treated, thus reducing their risks of subsequently succumbing to heart disease.

Obesity and overweight

Obesity is a risk factor for coronary heart disease in
itself. If you are overweight it is therefore important
that you don't compound your problems by having a
high blood cholesterol level, which is another risk
factor.

However, high cholesterol levels are often a consequence of consuming a diet too rich in saturated fats
and taking too little exercise, among other things. Such
a lifestyle will also tend to make you overweight. It
therefore follows that anyone who is overweight, and
particularly those who are severely overweight – obese
– will stand a good chance of having raised cholesterol
levels in their bloodstream, thus raising their chances of
subsequent coronary heart disease even higher. Tackling the weight problem should have the added bonus
of reducing cholesterol levels, thereby improving your
overall health at one go.

High blood pressure

High blood pressure is another risk factor in its own
right for coronary heart disease. If it is also coupled
with a raised blood cholesterol level, then the risks for
coronary heart disease are compounded. For anyone
who has been identified as suffering from high blood
pressure it is therefore important to clarify whether or
not they also have elevated circulating cholesterol
levels.

The picture may well be complicated by the fact that
drugs that are prescribed for the treatment of hyper-

tension (high blood pressure) can also elevate blood cholesterol levels. However, not all anti-hypertensive drugs have this effect, and by judicious prescription of the appropriate drugs it should be possible to establish whether or not the elevated cholesterol levels were caused by the drugs or by another problem.

Smoking

If you smoke heavily (over 20 a day) you already have a high risk of coronary heart disease. If you also have a high level of cholesterol circulating in the blood-stream, then your risk of coronary heart disease is increased disproportionately. It therefore behoves you to aim to reduce your cholesterol level and cut out the smoking.

Diabetes

Type II diabetics, in particular, tend to have raised blood cholesterol levels, and this puts them at an increased risk of coronary heart disease and of athero-sclerotic-related diseases such as a stroke.

If you are a diabetic, you will invariably have your blood glucose levels monitored. How well you are able to control your blood glucose levels will obviously depend on how well you comply to dietary, lifestyle and treatment regimes. Some diabetics are better at this than others, and some respond to such regimes better than others. However, because of this associated risk of elevated blood lipid levels, it is imperative that you also have your lipid levels monitored as well. Obviously the aim is then to keep your blood cholesterol levels within healthy limits; fortunately, the diet that is recom-mended to keep your blood glucose levels within safe limits will also help to control your blood lipid levels.

RISK FACTORS AND YOU

Having read this book so far, you should be well aware of what the various risk factors are for coronary heart disease. What should you do if you feel that one or more of these factors applies to you?

You are advised to go and see your doctor. Not only will he be able to have your blood cholesterol level measured, he will also be able to take into account all the other factors in your life, and advise you accordingly.

- If your total cholesterol level is found to be less than 5.2 mmol/l, and providing other risk factors such as obesity, high blood pressure, smoking, etc., are not a problem, then your doctor will probably tell you not to worry about it, although he might offer you advice on a healthy diet and lifestyle.
- If your total cholesterol level is found to be in the range of 5.2 to 6.5 mmol/l – a mild problem – your doctor will probably give you advice on diet, on exercise, on weight reduction if necessary, and if other risk factors, such as high blood pressure, are present, he will address these as well. There should be a follow-up check after 6 to 12 months.
- If your total cholesterol level is found to be over 6.5 mmol/l – a moderate or severe problem – a more rigorous treatment will be prescribed, especially if other risk factors are present. However, consideration of the HDL, LDL and triglyceride profile will have to be given before any firm decisions on treatment are made.

These levels, and the various responses you can expect to them on the part of your doctor, are examined in more detail in Chapter 10.

5

Changing your diet

The time has come to look at the practical implications of what we have been discussing. The current epidemic of coronary heart disease in the western industrialised countries is caused by the type of lifestyle we follow. In particular, high cholesterol levels appear to be one of the most serious, if not the most serious, risk factors; and one of the major causative factors in high blood cholesterol levels is a diet that contains a high proportion of fat in it, particularly what is known as saturated fat. This means that if you modify your diet so that you consume less fat, and in particular less saturated fat, you are actively reducing your chances of coronary heart disease.

One point does need to be made clear at the outset, though. All these statements are largely based on statistical conclusions, i.e. if a large group of people all adopt a lower-fat diet the incidence of coronary heart disease amongst them will be reduced. But this cannot be interpreted as saying that if you eat a low-fat diet you won't have coronary heart disease: it merely means that you reduce your chances of suffering from coronary heart disease. There is no way you can guarantee yourself no chance of having heart disease, just as there is no way you can guarantee not to be involved in a road accident. Modifying your diet – and your lifestyle – is about improving your chances of a healthy life.

But this is perhaps putting the cart before the horse, the conclusion at the beginning of the chapter. Let's first look at exactly what the constituents of our diet are.

CONSTITUENTS OF THE DIET

At its very simplest, food can be considered to consist of the following:

- Protein.
- Carbohydrate.
- Fats.
- Minerals and vitamins.
- Fibre.

Food also contains water, to a greater or lesser extent, but this need not concern us too much here, as it has no nutritional value.

Protein

The proteins in our food provide the basic building blocks in our body; they are intimately involved in the repair of old cells and in the manufacture of new cells. Protein largely consists of carbon, hydrogen, oxygen and nitrogen, with traces of other elements incorporated into different proteins. These elements form the amino acids – the basic units of protein structure – and different combinations and numbers of amino acids are

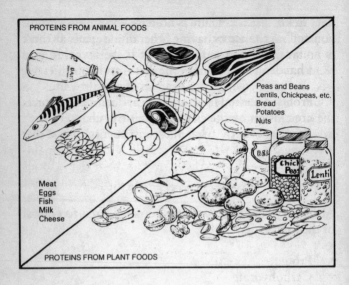

PROTEINS FROM ANIMAL FOODS

Peas and Beans
Lentils, Chickpeas, etc.
Bread
Potatoes
Nuts

Meat
Eggs
Fish
Milk
Cheese

PROTEINS FROM PLANT FOODS

Typical protein foods

linked together to construct different proteins. When we digest protein it is broken down into its constituent amino acids in the gut. These amino acids are then absorbed, processed and used in different parts of the body as and where necessary.

From this it should be apparent that it is essential that you consume enough protein – if you don't you are likely to suffer from malnutrition. However, you don't need as much in the way of protein as most people think; and if you consume an excess of protein, the surplus amino acids are utilised as a fuel to give energy or stored as body fat. Certainly in the west we are used to consuming far more protein than we need.

The only other detail we need know about protein is the distinction between high and low biological value protein (often called first and second class protein). The human body can actually synthesise amino acids itself, but not all the amino acids. The amino acids it can't manufacture are called the essential amino acids, and these have to be supplied in the diet.

- Proteins derived from animals and animal products are rich sources of essential amino acids.
- Proteins derived from plants often contain a lower proportion of the essential amino acids. To maintain your health while living only on plant foods you need to ensure a good mixture of different protein sources – beans with cereals, for example; this will help give you the correct range of essential amino acids.

Carbohydrate

Carbohydrate consists of the elements carbon, hydrogen and oxygen, and is used largely as an energy source. Like proteins, carbohydrates are broken down into small units in the gut, these units being known generally as sugars, of which the best known is glucose. What we know and buy as sugar – the sugar you get in bags in shops – is correctly known as sucrose and consists of two simple sugars, or units, called glucose and fructose.

We can distinguish between simple and complex carbohydrates:

- **Simple** carbohydrates are often found in highly refined foods, consisting of little or nothing else but carbohydrate, packet sugar (sucrose) being the best example. In the gut these simple carbohydrates are quickly broken down and flood into the bloodstream. Typical examples are sugar, syrup, honey, sweets, and the sugar found in many fruits (fructose).

- **Complex** carbohydrates, starch and dietary fibre are found in staple foods such as bread and other cereals, potatoes, and peas, beans and lentils (the pulses). In the gut these complex carbohydrates are broken down much more slowly, which is better for the body.

Once carbohydrates have been broken down in the gut into their basic units, these units pass into the bloodstream and are then transported around the body and used as energy sources wherever they are needed; in other words they are the fuel the body needs in order to function. However, if we take in too much of this fuel it is ultimately laid down as fat – the fat is simply an energy store.

Fats

Like carbohydrates, fats also consist of carbon, hydrogen and oxygen, but in different proportions. It is in fact more accurate to refer to this group as 'lipids', of which fats and oils are merely a subgroup. However, the only other lipid which need concern us here is cholesterol itself, which is a lipid but not an oil or fat. And don't be put off by the distinction between oils and fats; they are roughly the same thing, except that fats are solid at room temperature and oils are liquid.

The great majority of the fats we consume in the course of a day are what are called triglycerides. Each molecule of triglyceride, whatever the fat or oil it comes from, has the same basic structure:

- A three-pronged backbone of glycerol.

• Attached to each prong of the glycerol unit is a unit of fatty acid.

Thus the tri- prefix in the word triglyceride indicates that there are three fatty acid units per molecule.

The glycerol backbone in the molecule remains the same, whatever the fat or oil we are considering, but the fatty acids can vary widely, conferring different properties on the fats and oils. A fatty acid is basically a string of carbon atoms joined together, different fatty acids consisting of strings of different numbers of carbon atoms, and it is the number of carbon atoms in the fatty acids that, in part, give a fat or oil its characteristics.

However, there is another important characteristic of fatty acids. Each carbon atom has the ability to form four links or bonds with other atoms. In a chain-like

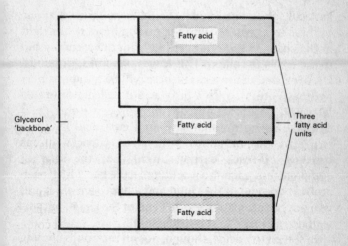

Basic structure of a triglyceride

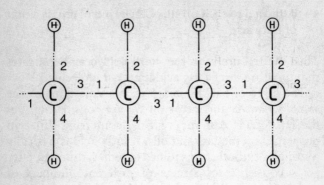

(C) — carbon atom

(H) — hydrogen atom

Bonding arrangement between carbon atoms in a fatty acid

molecule like a fatty acid it should be apparent that one of these links will be with the carbon atom to the right in the chain and another will be with the carbon atom to the left in the chain. This leaves two links, or bonds, left over, and in most cases these will be mopped up by hydrogen atoms. Such a fatty acid is called a saturated fatty acid, as it is saturated with hydrogen atoms, i.e. it can take up no more; a saturated fatty acid is thus a string of carbon atoms with two hydrogen atoms bristling off each carbon atom. (For the sake of completeness, each fatty acid molecule has a hydrogen atom at one end of the chain and a hydrogen atom and two oxygen atoms at the other end of the chain, but this is of no relevance to this discussion.)

In some fatty acids, though, not all the bonds coming off the carbon atoms in the chain are mopped up by hydrogen atoms; in these fatty acids, adjacent carbon

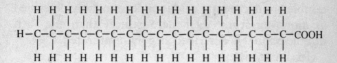

```
    H  H  H  H  H  H  H  H  H  H  H  H  H  H  H  H  H
    |  |  |  |  |  |  |  |  |  |  |  |  |  |  |  |  |
H – C– C– C– C– C– C– C– C– C– C– C– C– C– C– C– C– C– C– COOH
    |  |  |  |  |  |  |  |  |  |  |  |  |  |  |  |  |
    H  H  H  H  H  H  H  H  H  H  H  H  H  H  H  H  H
```

A saturated fatty acid, stearic acid, found for example in butter

```
    H  H  H  H  H  H  H  H  H              H  H  H  H  H
    |  |  |  |  |  |  |  |  |              |  |  |  |  |
H – C– C– C– C– C– C– C– C– C = C – C– C– C– C– C– C– C– C – COOH
    |  |  |  |  |  |  |  |                 |  |  |  |  |  |
    H  H  H  H  H  H  H  H                 H  H  H  H  H  H
```

A mono-unsaturated fatty acid, oleic acid, found for example in olive oil

```
    H  H  H  H  H  H  H  H  H  H  H  H  H  H  H  H
    |  |  |  |  |  |  |  |  |  |  |  |  |  |  |  |
H – C– C– C– C– C– C = C – C– C = C – C– C– C– C– C– C– C – COOH
    |  |  |  |  |        |        |  |  |  |  |  |  |
    H  H  H  H  H        H        H  H  H  H  H  H
```

A polyunsaturated fatty acid, linoleic acid, found for example in sunflower oil

```
    H  H  H  H  H  H  H  H  H  H  H  H  H  H  H  H
    |  |  |  |  |  |  |  |  |  |  |  |  |  |  |  |
H – C– C– C = C – C– C– C = C – C– C– C = C – C– C– C– C– C– C – COOH
    |  |        |        |        |  |  |  |  |  |  |
    H  H        H        H        H  H  H  H  H  H
```

Another polyunsaturated fatty acid, linolenic acid, found for example in soya oil

atoms in the chain are linked by two bonds. Where this occurs, the carbon atoms only have one bond left over for a hydrogen atom, and the fatty acid is described as being unsaturated, i.e. it has not taken up the maximum number of hydrogen atoms.

In an unsaturated fatty acid, by no means all the carbon atoms form such double bonds: there are usually only one or a few. If there is only one such double bond, the fatty acid is understandably described as mono-unsaturated; if there is more than one such double bond it is described as polyunsaturated.

To summarise:

- The great majority of the fats we eat are triglycerides.
- Each triglyceride molecule consists of a backbone of glycerol, to which are linked three fatty acids.
- Fatty acids can be saturated, mono-unsaturated or polyunsaturated, depending on the number of double bonds along their carbon chains.

So what happens when we eat some fat? The process of digestion in the gut breaks the triglycerides down into glycerol and free fatty acids, a process aided by the action of bile. The glycerol and fatty acid units are then small enough to pass across the gut wall into the bloodstream. During their passage across the gut wall these fatty acids and glycerol units are recombined into triglycerides, which are then taken in to the chylomicron particles in the bloodstream. You will remember from page 11 that the chylomicrons are just one of the lipoproteins, and that the lipoproteins in general consist of a fatty core – cholesterol and triglycerides – surrounded by apolipoprotein and phospholipid 'detergents'. And you may also remember that fatty acids are released from these chylomicrons as they pass around the body in the bloodstream, the released fatty acids being used as an energy source or, if not needed immediately, stored as fat.

Thus the fats we eat are either used as an energy source immediately or are laid down as fat stores, to be used as energy sources at a later date, should they be needed. In this respect fats are utilised in much the same way as carbohydrate, although the biochemistry is obviously different. But it must also be noted that fats are needed for the absorption of specific vitamins and to provide assorted fatty acids needed for cell structures and for hormone-like substances called prostaglandins.

Although the great bulk of the fats – or rather lipids – we eat are triglycerides, we do also consume a small amount of cholesterol. Dairy produce, offal (kidney, liver, etc.) egg yolk and some seafood are particularly rich in cholesterol. Such dietary cholesterol passes across the gut wall along with the glycerol and fatty acids, and is incorporated into the chylomicrons along with the resulting triglycerides.

Other nutrients

Nutritionally, this category is very important, and includes such essential dietary constituents as minerals and vitamins. The relationships between minerals, vitamins, cholesterol and coronary heart disease are important, but complex and beyond the scope of this book. A well-balanced diet with plenty of vegetables and fruit will provide the minerals and vitamins required.

Fibre

Much has been written about fibre in the last few years. The irony is that fibre is not a nutrient at all. By its very definition we don't digest fibre – it is not broken down and absorbed into the body. Instead it passes out of the digestive tract in largely the same form in which it is taken in.

Having said that, fibre is very important. Food and

the subsequent residues of digestion are moved along the digestive tract by a sort of muscular squeezing action. If we eat no fibre the food mass has little bulk to it – it is just a slushy mush – and this muscular squeezing action has nothing much to squeeze on. The result is that the food and its residues take far too long to pass through the digestive system, and various digestive and digestive-related disorders can result. Fibre is therefore essential in our diet to provide bulk and to give something for the digestive tract to grip on as its squeezes the food mass along.

It is important to distinguish between two sorts of dietary fibre.

- There is **insoluble** fibre, which is relatively inert, and merely adds a rough bulk to the food mass. Insoluble fibre is provided by many whole cereals such as wheat, rye and barley – wheat bran is perhaps the best known.
- Then there is **soluble** fibre, which is a softer sort of fibre, and has the important characteristic of being able to absorb water, helping to make the food mass softer and bulkier. Most fruit and vegetables contain soluble fibre, as do the legumes like lentils, chickpeas, kidney beans, peas, etc. Whole oats also provide soluble fibre, as to a lesser extent do other cereal foods.

FATS, CHOLESTEROL AND DIET

The question now is how does your diet – the protein, carbohydrate, fat and other nutrients we consume daily – affect the level of cholesterol circulating in your bloodstream?

It has already been pointed out that cholesterol is

actually produced in the body – in fact in all cells of the body, but chiefly in the liver and small intestine (see page 8). Someone who eats a vegan diet, with no meat or animal products whatsoever, still produces enough cholesterol to satisfy the needs of their body. But most of us don't eat a vegan diet – we eat a diet containing a lot of meat and meat products, a lot of dairy produce, a lot of eggs, and a lot of other fats, and these all contribute to the overall cholesterol level in the bloodstream.

- The dietary cholesterol we consume is one factor to be taken into consideration, although perhaps not as much as some books stress. Such cholesterol comes mainly from egg yolks, but also from meat – particularly offal meat – full fat milk, dairy products and some seafood.
- However the saturated fatty acids in our diet are an even more important factor, and can cause a build up of LDL cholesterol in the bloodstream. Such saturated fatty acids are derived from meat, especially meat products, full fat dairy produce and vegetable fats that have been processed ('hydrogenated') into margarine, and also include the vegetable oils palm and coconut oil (and therefore coconut itself).

In theory, the saturated fats and cholesterol we consume in our diet should shut down the body's synthesis of cholesterol, but this seems to be a mechanism that works better in some people than others.

Although the precise biochemical pathways linking dietary fat and circulating cholesterol levels are still in the process of elucidation, we do know that lowering our dietary intake of fat, and particularly of fats rich in saturated fatty acids, has a demonstrable effect in most people on levels of cholesterol circulating in the blood-stream.

REDUCTION OF DIETARY FATS

This section will look at the proportions of the various nutrients consumed in an 'average' western diet, and will then examine what proportions we ought to aim for if we want to have a healthy diet. But first, it would be useful to clarify some terminology, in particular exactly what a kilocalorie is, as it's a term that often crops up in discussions on diet.

The kilocalorie

The kilocalorie is a convenient measure of the amount of energy contained within a substance. Taken literally, it indicates the amount of energy that substance would liberate if it was burned as a fuel. It ought to be noted that kilocalories are often abbreviated in the media to calories, or to Calories; strictly speaking, it is an incorrect terminology, but is probably too ingrained in the public's mind to change overnight. You might also come across the energy value of food expressed in kilojoules (kJ) or megajoules MJ; 1 kilocalorie is 4.2 kJ, and 1,000 kilocalories are 4.2 MJ.

Our food is our fuel, so in the case of food the kilocalorie gives a measure of the amount of chemical energy that can be released after the food has been ingested and broken down within the body. High calorie foods are thus those foods that are energy dense, meaning that much energy will be released from relatively small amounts once they have been broken down within the body.

We use a certain amount of energy each day – the more active we are, the more energy we use. If we take in more energy, as measured by the kilocalories available in the food we eat, than we need then we put on weight; the surplus energy we take in is not used and is therefore laid down as a future store of energy, i.e. fat. Conversely, if we use more energy than we take in, we lose weight by using up our fat stores to supply our energy needs.

The four major food groups supply the following amounts of energy:

- 1 gram of fat   9 kilocalories
- 1 gram of protein   4 kilocalories
- 1 gram of carbohydrate 4 kilocalories
- 1 ml of alcohol   7 kilocalories

It is easy to see that, weight for weight, fats supply far more energy than the other nutrients, e.g. 100 grams (about 4 oz) of fat will supply 900 kilocalories while 100 grams of carbohydrate will supply 400 kilocalories. Therefore eating a diet rich in fats (and alcoholic drinks) will provide a lot of energy – invariably far more than is needed, which is why so many of us are overweight. A diet low in fat will therefore not only tend to lower the cholesterol level in the blood but will also automatically reduce the number of kilocalories taken in and thus help in weight reduction.

Reduction of total fat

It has been calculated that the average western diet yields about 40 per cent of its energy from fat. This is not to say that 40 per cent of the diet consists of fat, though. The important fact here is that fat contributes over twice as much energy, gram for gram, as carbohydrate and protein, so a smaller portion of fatty food will contribute more in the way of energy than a comparatively larger portion that is largely carbohydrate. For example, you might know that bacon, eggs and fried bread are pretty rich and fatty; you like them all the same, but to salve your conscience you only have one rasher of bacon, one egg and half a slice of bread. You then talk to a colleague at work, who says they have a huge bowl of porridge for breakfast. You feel pretty smug and self-satisfied because you've had a relatively tiny breakfast while your colleague has obviously stuffed himself. Such smugness would be ill-founded, though. The egg, bacon and greasy fried bread is extremely energy-rich, largely because of the high proportion of fat it contains, while the porridge contains relatively little energy (provided, of course, that you don't pour cream all over it).

As a very rough rule of thumb, if 20 per cent of your diet consists of fat, then 40 per cent of your energy supply will be fat based. Such a proportion is very easy to achieve when you remember that fat not only occurs on fatty meat; butter and margarine are largely fat, and both occur in pastry, cakes and biscuits, while milk, cheese and eggs all have a high fat content.

If, instead of 20 per cent of your diet consisting of fat, you reduced your fat intake to about 15 per cent, there would be two immediate consequences:

- You would immediately reduce the energy supplied by fat to about 30 per cent of the total.
- You would probably reduce your total energy intake, as you would be hard put to eat enough carbohydrate to keep the energy supply up to the previous total – for every gram of fat not eaten, you

would have to eat 2 grams of carbohydrate (or protein) to supply the same amount of energy.

Therefore, if you reduced your total fat intake you would reduce your overall energy intake. This would probably mean that you'd lose weight; you'd certainly stand much less chance of gaining weight. Of equal importance is the fact that saturated fatty acids appear to raise the level of cholesterol in the bloodstream.

This figure of less than 30 per cent of our energy to be supplied by fats is important for cholesterol lowering. It is also a good target to aim for in order to control weight and to promote good health generally.

Reduction of saturated fats

The reduction of total fat content of the diet is not the only important factor. In particular we need to cut back on our intake of saturated fats – those fats that contain saturated fatty acids. The evidence all points to the fact that it is the amount of saturated fatty acids we consume that has the most significant effect on our circulating cholesterol levels.

So, where do we get saturated fatty acids from in our diet? Well, they are largely animal-derived, i.e. if you eat no animal products you immediately reduce your chances of taking in saturated fats. Vegetarians sometimes consume low amounts of saturated fatty acids, although if they eat a lot of dairy produce – milk, cheese, etc. – and eggs this is not the case; vegans, who eat no animal produce whatsoever, stand a much better chance of consuming less saturated fatty acids.

But there are some saturated fats of vegetable origin – coconut and coconut products, for example, and palm kernel oil. In addition, the processing of vegetable oils to make margarine also results in the production of saturated fatty acids. The key phrase to look out for is 'hydrogenated vegetable oil'; this means that the poly-unsaturated vegetable oils have had hydrogen incorporated into their molecular structure so that they become saturated – hydrogenated in this case means saturated.

It is impossible to give a detailed breakdown of all those dietary items that are rich in saturated fat, but some guidelines are as follows:

- Fatty cuts of meat.
- Animal skin, e.g. bacon rind, chicken skin.
- Most processed meats, e.g. sausages, pâtes, salamis, luncheon meats.
- Cream and full-fat (ordinary silver-top) milk.
- Butter and many margarines.
- Suet, lard and dripping.
- Full-fat yogurt.
- Full-fat cheeses, e.g. Cheddar.
- Pastries, biscuits, cakes, puddings, etc., made with margarine rich in saturated fats, with butter, with milk, cream, etc.
- Foods fried in saturated fats.

'What is there left to eat?' you might be asking. For a start, there are many reduced-fat alternatives to items on the above list, and there are many other alternatives that are not high in saturated fatty acids. It is perfectly possible to have a diet that is low in fat, and in particular low in saturated fat, while still having a varied and tasty – and certainly not boring – range of meals.

The importance of MUFAs

MUFA is merely the abbreviation for mono-unsaturated fatty acid, and is a bit less of a mouthful to say. But why are MUFAs important?

The biochemical basis for their importance has not been elicited at the moment, but from various studies it appears that mono-unsaturated fatty acids tend to lower LDL while keeping HDL cholesterol levels raised. So if you switch to a diet that is low in saturated fats and high, relatively speaking, in MUFAs, you will reduce your levels of LDL cholesterol in your blood and keep your levels of HDL cholesterol up. As it is LDL cholesterol that is the principal risk factor for coronary heart disease, and HDL cholesterol actually protects against heart disease by removing cholesterol from atherosclerotic deposits, this can only be a good thing.

Some authorities have even gone so far as to suggest that a diet rich in MUFAs, providing other fatty acids are kept to a minimum, will lower total cholesterol levels and LDL cholesterol levels while keeping HDL cholesterol levels up. This does seem to be the case with a Mediterranean diet, so a sensible course of action would be to reduce the total fat content of the diet to 30 per cent of energy intake (about 15 per cent by weight), as explained above, and to try and ensure that MUFAs – mono-unsaturated fatty acids – make up the lion's share of this reduced fat content.

But where can you get MUFAs? The richest source of MUFAs is olive oil. Indeed, there is now much media coverage of the healthy benefits of using olive oil, the low incidence of coronary heart disease in the Mediterranean areas (where they use lots of olive oil) being quoted as the basis for this supposition. The problem is that olive oil is very expensive, and furthermore it has a distinctive taste which may be out of place in recipes other than salads and savoury dishes. Lighter versions of olive oil are now available, with a much milder flavour, but there are two other oils that are rich in MUFAs and are readily available – peanut and rapeseed oil; neither is as expensive as olive oil, and they certainly don't have such a distinctive taste. MUFAs also occur in avocados and peanuts.

What about PUFAs?

PUFAs are polyunsaturated fatty acids. And the majority of recent advice has been that we should cut back on fat intake, and substitute polyunsaturated fats for saturated fats within this reduced fat intake. But if the authorities are not recommending an emphasis on MUFAs, what should we do about PUFAs? Should we forget about them completely?

The answer to the last question appears to be a definite no. Polyunsaturated fats provide important constituents of the diet – some of the polyunsaturated fatty acids are in fact essential. The advice is therefore to reduce the overall intake of fat, to try and ensure that mono-unsaturated fatty acids constitute a significant proportion of this reduced fat content, with polyunsaturated fatty acids taking up the next largest share.

There has been plenty of advice on what food products contain levels of PUFAs. The consumer has been bombarded with advice about the benefits of polyunsaturates, and whole sections of our shops and supermarkets are stuffed with manufactured products labelled 'high in polyunsaturates' – cooking fats and oils, particularly those rich in sunflower and safflower oils, yellow spreads to be used instead of butter, foods cooked with fats and oils rich in PUFAs. It is less widely known that oily fish and nuts are good sources of PUFAs.

What is essential to remember, though, is that any change in diet to lower cholesterol levels should, as a first step, involve a reduction in total fat intake. By all means switch from butter to a polyunsaturate-rich spread, but you are going to gain little (if any) benefit if you then slap this PUFA-rich spread on to your bread or toast so that it's half an inch thick.

Reduction of cholesterol intake

So far we have talked about lowering blood cholesterol levels by reducing our fat intake, and, within this reduced-fat diet, putting a preference first on mono-unsaturated fats, then on polyunsaturated fats and, last of all, on saturated fats. The reason behind this advice is based in large part on the fact that saturated fats play by far the major dietary role in determining blood cholesterol levels.

There is debate within the medical world as to how much dietary cholesterol intake also affects blood cholesterol levels. It certainly doesn't have an impact on cholesterol levels as much as the saturated fat intake. However, if we want to lower blood cholesterol levels we do need to keep an eye on dietary cholesterol intake, for the simple reason that dietary cholesterol is usually found in foods that also contain significant proportions of saturated fats. And dietary cholesterol comes from:

- Eggs, the yolks containing all the cholesterol.
- Organ meat, such as liver, kidney, heart.
- Butter and many hard cheeses such as Cheddar and Stilton.

Seafoods such as crab, lobster and shrimp also contain significant proportions of cholesterol, but they are associated with high levels of polyunsaturated fats, so should not figure on a 'banned' list – although, given their price, they're not the sort of food you're likely to be eating every day. And because of their relatively high cholesterol content they should certainly be limited items in a low-fat diet.

Advice on fats – summary

- Reduce the fat intake – it should comprise about 30 per cent of the energy intake of the diet, which translates as about 15 per cent of the intake by weight. This is the most important piece of advice.
- Of the fats consumed, mono-unsaturates should comprise the major proportion; aim for mono-unsaturates comprising half the total of fats, if possible.
- Polyunsaturates should comprise the next largest proportion of fats.
- saturated fats should comprise the smallest proportion of fats; reducing the consumption of saturated fats is the other important piece of advice.
- Aim to keep the cholesterol intake low.

INCREASE COMPLEX CARBOHYDRATES

If you are going to cut down on your fat intake, with what, if anything, are you going to replace it? The simple answer is complex carbohydrates, such as fruit, vegetables and cereals. Six to eight portions a day are easily achieved if you have cereal for breakfast, potato and a second vegetable with your main meal, some fruit or salad with another meal, and perhaps a piece of fruit as a snack at some other time in the day. But remember, full-fat milk on cereals and butter or cream on vegetables or fruit add to the intake of saturated fat, as do most sauces, custards, etc.

Complex carbohydrates also occur in other forms as well. Cereals, such as rice and pasta, are good examples. Peas and beans – baked beans, red kidney beans, split peas, chickpeas, lentils, etc. – are good sources of complex carbohydrate and contain valuable protein, so they can be used as alternatives to meat in menu planning. Wholemeal flour could be incorporated into recipes instead of plain flour, for extra fibre.

The overall effect of increasing the intake of complex carbohydrate is to provide over half of the energy needs from carbohydrate and to ensure that as large a proportion as possible of the carbohydrate consists of starchy foods. Meals based on this premise will be substantial, because of the bulk associated with filling complex carbohydrates. Furthermore, because such carbohydrate takes time to digest, the bloodstream does not receive sudden surges of simple sugars like glucose; instead the products of digestion appear in the bloodstream over a period of time.

INCREASE THE FIBRE INTAKE

If you increase your intake of complex carbohydrates at the same time as reducing your fat intake, particularly your saturated fat intake, it will automatically follow that you will increase your intake of fibre.

As we saw earlier in the chapter, there are two types of fibre in food, insoluble fibre and soluble fibre. If you are aiming to reduce your cholesterol levels it is particularly important that you get an adequate supply

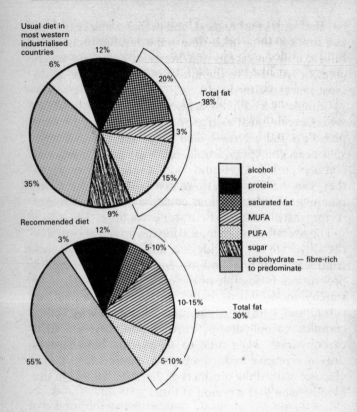

The proportions of the diet, by energy content (not weight), in a typical western country and in the recommended low-fat cholesterol lowering diet

of soluble fibre in your diet. The reasoning behind this is as follows. You will remember from Chapter 2 that the bulk of the cholesterol our bodies synthesise each day ends up in bile – the bile is produced in the liver, stored in the gallbladder and released into the gut to help with fat digestion. The bile salts then pass down the gut into the large intestine, where they are resorbed and recycled into cholesterol. Soluble fibre, far from being inert like insoluble fibre, can absorb water and bind other chemicals to it, including these bile salts. Thus, as the soluble fibre passes along the gut, it mops up some of the bile salts and prevents them from being resorbed in the large intestine. They are then passed out in the faeces and are thus removed from what might be termed the 'cholesterol cycle'. The overall level of cholesterol circulating in the bloodstream is in this way reduced – a simple yet elegant method.

Soluble fibre is found, to a greater or lesser extent, in all fresh fruit and vegetables, but a rich source are the legume vegetables or pulses – peas and beans. In particular, the legumes such as split peas, lentils, chickpeas, red kidney beans, haricot beans, etc., and including baked beans, are all very rich sources of soluble fibre. From this it should be apparent that cooking with beans, lentils, chickpeas, etc., can only be a good thing if you want to reduce your cholesterol level:

- They are a good source of protein, so can be substituted for meat, thus reducing the intake of saturated fat.
- They are a good source of complex carbohydrate.
- They are a good source of soluble fibre, which removes bile salts from the 'cholesterol cycle'.

Another good source of soluble fibre is oats, and it is recommended that oats and oatmeal be incorporated into the diet wherever is reasonable. Oat bran is the part of the oat grain that is richest in oat fibre, and this can be used as an addition to many recipes, and will

certainly help in the effect soluble fibre has on cholesterol levels. A more detailed examination of oat bran
occurs in Chapter 8.

FISH AND SEAFOOD

There is one simple reason for eating fish and seafood
instead of meat, and that is because fish is rich in
polyunsaturated fatty acids, whereas meat is rich in
saturated fatty acids. However, there is a more potent
reason for eating fish.

Fish in general contain polyunsaturated fatty acids
that are not found in plants – as one might expect. But
cold-water seafish, in particular, contain a group of
polyunsaturated fatty acids that give rise to products
that seem to have a positive protective effect against
coronary heart disease. For a start, the passage of
cholesterol-rich blood cells into the wall of the artery in
the very early stages of atherosclerosis seems to be
reduced by these products. Then, later in the development of the atherosclerotic deposits, the formation of a
'clot' on top of the deposits is also limited – the blood
itself is rendered less 'sticky' and less liable to clot
(which, carried to extremes, can pose problems of its
own).

Eating fish and seafood in general is therefore to be
recommended as part of a policy of reducing the intake
of saturated fats. Furthermore, eating cold-water oily
seafish such as mackerel, herring and salmon appears
to be positively beneficial. What is not recommended is
that you deep-fry or fry the fish, thus adding more fat
during the cooking process – and fish and chips has an
extremely high fat content associated with it as a result
of the deep fat frying of both the fish and the potatoes.

EXTRA LOW-FAT DIET

The recommendations given so far apply not only to those who need or want to lower their blood cholesterol levels. These guidelines can also be recommended as the basis for a healthy diet in general.

But what happens if you need to be on an extra low-fat diet, perhaps because you have familial hyper-cholesterolaemia and have an excessively high blood cholesterol level and associated risk of coronary heart disease. In such a situation it is a question of adopting the same sort of diet that has been suggested already, but adhering to the suggestions more stringently. For many such people, drug therapy will also be necessary, but the low-fat, low-saturated-fat diet will underpin any such treatment.

HOW EASY IS IT?

For someone who eats a lot of wholefoods and fresh fruit and vegetables, and who understand the links between diet and good health, these suggestions for changing the daily diet to control blood cholesterol levels will not seem onerous. They might miss the clotted cream on their porridge, or the suet dumplings with the beef and lentil hotpot, but they will know that a low-fat, complex-carbohydrate-rich diet need not be bland and boring.

But the chances are that someone who suddenly discovers they have a high cholesterol level will not have been much bothered about their diet. If they've been used to a lot of convenience foods, a lot of fast foods, a lot of fried food, they will find it very difficult changing their diet and cutting all of those out, particularly if their work colleagues or their family continue on a high fat diet.

It is important that they get a lot of explanation as to why it is necessary to change their diet and a lot of help and advice on how it is to be achieved. First of all they have to be motivated to change, and then they need careful and sympathetic help to achieve such a change.

On the accompanying pages is a chart that lists the foods that can be eaten regularly; these are in the two left-hand columns. Choose your foods from these columns to create healthy menus of low fat, low saturated fat and low cholesterol meals. Foods in the third column may be higher in fat and cholesterol and may also be higher in sugar and salt. Choose from this column only occasionally. Eating foods from column four is not a good idea if you have a high blood lipid level; an occasional lapse may not do any great harm, but regularly choosing foods from this column is to be discouraged.

Such a chart is a good starting point for change. But it ought to be backed up with a lot of help and support from the GP, dietitian and other people. If somebody else usually cooks and shops for you, they should also be involved, as they will be the agent of change in your dietary habits.

It is also important to realise that sudden changes can't be expected in your diet. First you need to accept the need for change; until that is accepted, modifications to the diet are likely to be slight and/or transient. However, once you have accepted the change is necessary you are halfway there; you will start to experiment, or will accept experiments, and will start to seek out alternative products and foods.

What is essential is to realise that a low-fat healthy diet is not bland, is not boring, is not time-consuming in its preparation and can be very interesting. In the following chapter we give some practical advice that underlines these facts.

	The Best Choices		Occasional Additions	Look left for better choices
	Contain least fat, salt, sugar	*Contain a little fat, salt, sugar*	*Contain more fat, salt, sugar*	*Contain too much fat, salt, sugar*
Staple foods	Cereals bread, chapatti (*low fat*), oats, pasta, porridge, rice, all other cereals	Cereals bread (*with a scrape of fatty spread*), pancake, scone, tea cake	Cereals bread (*with fatty spread*), chapatti (*made with fat*), iced bread, papadum, paratha, fried rice	Cereals bread, *fried*
	Potato baked, boiled or instant, sweet potato (yam)	Potato mashed (*with a little milk or fat*), oven or thick chips (*in unsaturated vegetable oil*), roast (*in unsaturated vegetable oil*)	Potato croquettes, waffles (*oven baked*), *low fat crisps*	Potato chips (*thin or crinkle cut*), crisps
	Pulses beans, dahl, lentils, peas			
		Pasta *canned in sauce*	Pastry made with unsaturated fat	Pastry including croissant and Danish
		Breakfast cereals *not sugar coated*	Breakfast cereals *sugar coated*	
Vegetables and Fruits	Vegetables canned, dried, fresh, frozen including beans, lentils, peas	Vegetables *bottled or canned in a sauce*, coleslaw (*in low fat dressing*), stirfry vegetables, hummus, soup (*home-made, not 'cream of'*)	Vegetables *fried in unsaturated fat*, soup (*canned or packet*)	Vegetables *with butter or other fat added, or fried in saturated fat*, coleslaw or other salad in undetermined dressing
	Fruits *canned in natural juice*, dried, fresh, frozen	Fruits avocado, olive, others stewed *with minimal sugar*	Fruits *canned in syrup*	Fritters

Meats and Alternatives			
Meat very lean cuts of beef, chicken, game, ham, pork, turkey, veal	Meat lean cuts of lamb and other meats, corned beef, oxtail, stewed steak (canned with gravy)	Meat lean mince, offal, heart, kidney, liver, sweetbreads, tongue, tripe, low fat burgers, low fat sausages	Meat products such as black/white pudding, burgers, canned luncheon meat, faggots, goose, haggis, sausage rolls, scotch eggs, sausage meat, poultry with visible fat and skin or breaded and fried
White fish cod, haddock, plaice	Oily fish pilchards, sardines, herring, mackerel, salmon, trout, tuna	Fish anchovies, smoked mackerel, any fish battered or bread crumbed if fried in unsaturated fat	Fish white bait, roe, taramasalata, fried fish or fish products in saturated fat
Molluscs cockles, mussels, whelks		Shellfish prawn, shrimp, crab, lobster	
Pulses beans, dahl, lentils, peas			
Meat substitutes Quorn or tofu	Meat substitutes texturised vegetable protein (TVP)		
Nuts chestnuts		Nuts all nuts other than chestnuts and coconut	Nuts coconut
Egg whites		Eggs boiled, poached no added fat	Egg yolk (more than four per week), fried, omelette, scrambled

Foods for Extra Calcium			
Milk skimmed, Soya	Milk semi skimmed, flavoured milks	Milk condensed skimmed, evaporated, goat, sheep, whole	Milk condensed, whole, dried (with added vegetable fat), cream, creme fraiche
Cheeses low fat varieties of cottage, curd, fromage frais	Cheeses reduced fat varieties of fromage frais, hard, slices, soft, spreads	Cheeses full fat varieties of fromage frais, hard, slices, soft, spreads	Cheeses cream cheese
Yoghurt very low fat/low calorie	Yoghurt low fat	Yoghurt soya, whole milk	Yoghurt Greek

	Contain least fat, salt, sugar	Contain a little fat, salt, sugar	Contain more fat, salt, sugar	Contain too much fat, salt, sugar
Composite Dishes	Savoury potato crust 'pies' with fish, vegetable or lean meat filling, shepherds pie, hotpot, Irish stew, pizza (with low fat topping), chow mein, kedgeree, paella, pasta (with tomato based sauce) Desserts fruit (baked or stewed), fruit fools or syllabubs made with low fat fromage frais/yoghurt), jelly (low sugar)	Savoury cauliflower cheese, chilli con carne, curry, dim sum (steamed), lasagne, macaroni cheese, moussaka, tikka recipes Low fat recipe meals	Savoury pies one crust only, pasta in cream sauce, Welsh rarebit Desserts fruit crumble, fruit pie (one thin pastry crust only), fruit trifle, fruit flan, milk pudding, custard, rice, sago, semolina, tapioca, tray bakes or cakes using suitable ingredients	Savoury dim sum (fried), 'en-croute' recipes, pies (two pastry crusts), quiche, samosa, suet dumplings and puddings Desserts tray bakes or cakes using hard fats
Oils and Fats	Small quantities of: see next column	Spreads (very low fat, low fat and reduced fat), margarine (unsaturated used sparingly) Oils unsaturated of named origin such as sunflower, corn, olive, rapeseed but used sparingly	Spreads peanut butter Salad dressings reduced fat or home-made with suitable ingredients	Spreads not labelled 'high in unsaturates', hard margarine, butter products, ghee Cooking fats dripping, lard, suet Salad dressings mayonnaise (full fat)

Drinks	Water, mineral water, tea, coffee (*freshly made*), milk *skimmed or Soya*	Juice *unsweetened* fruit or vegetable juices Squash and fizzy pop (*low calorie*) Alcohol *low alcohol drinks*	Juice *sweetened* fruit juice Squash and fizzy pop (*standard*) Alcohol Milky drinks malted milk, hot chocolate (*made with low fat milk or water*) Yoghurt drink	Coffee whitener, white coffee *from vending machines* Alcohol cream based liqueurs
Cakes and Biscuits	Biscuits crisp breads, Matzos, rice cakes, water biscuits	Cakes *low fat and reduced sugar*	Biscuits cereal bars, fig roll, garibaldi, ginger, jaffa cake, plain semi sweet, home made tray bakes (*with suitable ingredients*), meringue, oatcakes, sponge fingers, wholemeal crackers	Biscuits *cream filled*, shortbread Savoury nibbles Cakes commercially produced, lardy cake, doughnuts
Flavourings	Condiments herbs, lemon juice, mustard, pepper, Tabasco, vinegar, garlic, tomato purée Artificial sweetener	Condiments brown sauce, chutney, horseradish, ketchup, pickle, soy, stock cubes, salt substitutes, stuffing mix (*packet*), Worcestershire sauce, other sauces (*canned and packet*)	Condiments Bovril, gravy granules, Marmite	Condiments salt

6

Practical help with diet

Now has come the time to turn some of the generalisations encountered in the previous pages into practical tips and advice so that you can create a tasty and interesting diet that is low on fat, and particularly saturated fats, and low on cholesterol, and be well on the way to a healthy diet.

MENUS FOR A WEEK

To many people the idea of a low-fat diet means a boring diet, but this need not be the case. To give you some idea as to just how tasty and interesting such a diet can be we have drawn up a sample menu list for a week's meals. You can either follow the programme right through one week, or pick and choose the ideas that appeal to you.

Monday

Breakfast   Oat cereal and skimmed milk
Toast, low-fat spread and jam, honey or marmalade

Lunch	Rice cakes
	Low-fat cheese, hard or soft
	Tomatoes and onion, chopped finely
	Apple
Dinner	Chilli con carne, made with lean meat
	Rice, boiled
	Green salad
	Low-fat yoghurt

Tuesday

Breakfast	Bran flakes and small banana, chopped
	Skimmed milk
Lunch	Pasta shell salad, made with red and green peppers, onions, chickpeas, kidney beans, tomatoes and lean diced ham
	Roll with a little low-fat spread
Dinner	Chicken casserole
	Boiled potatoes
	Lemon sorbet

Wednesday

Breakfast	Oat cereal with skimmed milk and stewed apple
	Toast with low-fat spread
Lunch	Baked beans on toast
	Low-fat yoghurt
	Orange
Dinner	Grilled kipper
	Tomatoes, peas and boiled potatoes in their skins
	Banana

Thursday

Breakfast	Porridge made with skimmed milk
	Stewed apple on top
Lunch	Sandwich/roll/bap with low-fat spread

	Filling consisting of salad mix, e.g. lettuce, low-fat cheese, tomatoes, onion, pepper, mustard and cress
	Fruit with *fromage frais*
Dinner	Spaghetti bolognese made with lean mince, tomato purée, onions, grated carrot, pinch of mixed herbs, on top of wholemeal spaghetti
	Low-fat yoghurt

Friday

Breakfast	Oat cereal with skimmed milk
	Wholemeal toast, low-fat spread and marmalade, jam or honey
Lunch	Rice salad with tuna, onions, red kidney beans, peppers, lettuce, all mixed with plain *fromage frais*
	Rye bread/crispbread/crackers and low-fat spread
	Yoghurt
Dinner	Cauliflower in low-fat cheese sauce, topped with toasted breadcrumbs
	Boiled carrots and jacket baked potato
	Date slice

Saturday

Breakfast	Porridge with skimmed milk and a small chopped banana
Lunch	Ratatouille with jacket baked potato/rice/pasta
	Apple or orange
Dinner	Vegetable quiche (a small portion)
	Mixed salad, with no dressing or a little olive oil dressing
	Bread and low-fat spread
	Rice pudding made with skimmed milk

Sunday

Breakfast   Low-fat plain yoghurt/*fromage frais*/cottage cheese

Toast with low-fat spread and marmalade/jam/honey/yeast extract

Lunch   Lean roast meat

Jacket potato/boiled potatoes in skins

Lightly steamed/boiled green vegetables

Oat-topped fruit crumble with low-fat yoghurt

Supper   Sandwich with low-fat soft cream cheese and banana filling

Apple or orange

SHOPPING LIST

To cook or prepare the meals in the week's menu list above you need to get the items below and on the following page. As well as helping you prepare the meals we have outlined, this shopping list will also give you an idea of the sort of items you ought to be buying if you are on a low-fat, cholesterol-lowering diet.

- Skimmed milk
- Low-fat spread
- Pure sunflower oil margarine, or one labelled high in mono-unsaturates or polyunsaturates
- Natural and fruit low-fat yoghurts
- Low-fat *fromage frais*
- Low-fat cottage cheese
- Low-fat hard and soft cheeses
- Eggs (to be used sparingly) or egg replacer such as Loprofin, available in healthfood stores and some chemists

- Olive oil (or another oil high in mono-unsaturates)
- Very lean minced beef
- Meat for roasting – very lean, with visible fat removed
- Lean ham
- Oily fish, e.g. mackerel, sardines, herring, salmon, trout
- Tinned tuna
- Oat bran
- Rolled oats
- Bran flakes
- Oat cereal
- Rice
- Pasta
- Bread and rolls/baps
- Rye bread/crispbread/crackers
- Rice cakes
- Fresh/frozen vegetables
- Baking potatoes
- Salad ingredients
- Tinned tomatoes
- Beans, chickpeas and red kidney beans
- Baked beans
- Tomato purée
- Dried/fresh herbs
- Apples for stewing
- Other fresh fruit, including a lemon and bananas
- Dried fruit, e.g. raisins, dates, apricots
- Lemon sorbet
- Honey
- Jams/marmalades
- Yeast extract, e.g. Marmite

RECIPES AND COOKING TIPS

In this section are some general ideas for cooking low-fat meals, along with some specific recipes for dishes listed in the week's sample menu list, particularly those dishes you might not have come across before.

Meat

- When cooking red meat always trim off as much fat as possible.
- When cooking chicken or turkey, remove the skin before cooking and wrap in foil to prevent the breast-meat drying out.
- You can bake, roast, grill or fry meat slowly without any added fat, allowing its own juices to do the job. When cooked slowly in this way it won't dry up or go tough.
- When cooking casseroles, stews, chilli con carne, spaghetti sauces, meat pie fillings, or whatever, reduce the amount of meat that's in the recipe and add a can of ready-prepared pulses, e.g. red kidney beans, butter beans, chick peas. This cuts back on the saturated fat, increases the vegetable fibre content, provides a very nutritious and tasty meal and is cheaper.
- If you're making a stew or a casserole you can reduce the fat content even further by making it a day in advance and then skimming off the fat once it has cooled – either use a spoon or a spatula, or pull a paper towel across the surface if the fat is still warm.
- Roast joints of meat should be cooked on a rack/cooking tray to allow any fat to drain away.

Spaghetti bolognese

Everyone has heard of this recipe, but few know how to make it properly. Its true name is *ragu*, and it ought to be made with minced lean beef, chicken livers and bacon or uncooked ham. From our point of view this combination is obviously not acceptable, so here is an excellent variation in line with the needs of a low-fat diet. (For two to four people.)

8 oz (225 g) lean minced beef
1 onion, chopped
1 carrot, sliced finely
1 piece of celery, sliced finely
3 tsp of tomato purée
1 wineglass of white wine
½ pint (300 ml) non-fatty stock or water
seasoning

Use a tiny amount of olive oil to fry the chopped onion, carrot and celery. When they have softened add the mince and stir until the meat is well browned; if you are dubious about the leanness of the meat you could strain any fat off at this stage, or allow it to cool and lift the fat off by drawing a piece of kitchen paper over the top of the mixture.

Bring the mixture back to the heat, stir in the tomato purée and the wine; add the stock or water and season to taste. Cover and simmer for half an hour to an hour, by which time the sauce should be rich and thick.

Cook the pasta, drain and tip into a serving bowl, then toss in the sauce, allowing it to coat the spaghetti thoroughly. Serve immediately.

Variations include adding some grated nutmeg with the

seasoning, and stirring in a little flour after you have added the mince if you find the sauce is too thin. Garlic is also often added with the meat, or various herbs such as a bouquet garni. You can experiment to please your own taste buds.

Fish

- White fish can be simply baked in the oven, without the requirement of a rich sauce. Just brush the fish lightly with a little unsaturated oil before putting it in the oven.
- Oily fish can be grilled slowly, without the need to add any extra fat. This applies equally well to kippers and other smoked fish.
- Another way to bake fish is to wrap it, either filleted or merely deheaded and gutted, in aluminium foil, along with some slices of tomato and onion and a few herbs. Then place it in a hot oven for about half an hour so that it cooks in its own juices.

Pasta shell salad

Pasta, cooked and allowed to cool, can be used as the basis for a wide variety of salads. Here is a typical example for four people.

4–6 oz (100–175 g) pasta
1 small red and 1 small green pepper
1 small onion
4 oz (100 g) chickpeas/red kidney beans, cooked
4 tomatoes
4 oz (100 g) lean ham, diced (optional)
seasoning

Cook the wholemeal pasta, drain, pour on a little olive oil and mix (to stop the pasta sticking), then leave to cool.

Chop the vegetables finely and stir them and the chick peas/red kidney beans and diced ham into the pasta. Add seasoning, herbs and garlic as preferred.

You might find that a dressing is not needed. If you want to add a dressing, use a small amount of a simple olive oil and vinegar dressing, or some low-fat yoghurt and a little squeeze of lemon juice.

Pastry

One easy way to introduce more soluble fibre into your diet is to make pastry incorporating some oat bran. This gives the pastry a lovely nutty flavour that the whole family will appreciate.

6 oz (175 g) flour
2 oz (50 g) oat bran
4 oz (100 g) vegetable fat low in saturates
water to mix
pinch of salt if preferred

Mix together the flour and oat bran (and salt if desired) in a large bowl. Rub in the vegetable fat until the mixture resembles fine breadcrumbs. Sprinkle the water on to the mixture – just enough to make a soft dough. Wrap in clingfilm and place in the refrigerator for 20 minutes. Then roll out as usual.

An alternative to this is a delicious oat pastry. Besides tasting excellent this has the added bonus of being very low in saturated fat and very high in soluble fibre.

8 oz (225 g) rolled oats

6 tbsp peanut oil
water to mix
pinch of salt if desired

Mix the ingredients together as described above. Then press the mixture into a medium-sized flan dish.

Low-fat vegetable quiche

8 oz (225 g) oat pastry
1 carrot, grated
small red, green and yellow peppers, diced
1 large onion, chopped
2 oz (50 g) mushrooms, chopped
2–3 tomatoes, sliced
½ pint (300 ml) skimmed milk + 2 egg whites beaten together
OR 1 packet of silken tofu, beaten
herbs and seasoning to taste

Line a medium-sized flan dish with greaseproof paper, or merely grease the dish. Roll out the pastry and use to line the dish. Bake the pastry case blind at 200 °C (400°F, gas mark 6) for 15 minutes. Sprinkle the prepared vegetables around the inside of the pastry case, then pour over the milky mixture or the tofu. Bake in a hot oven (190 °C, 375 °F, gas mark 5) for about half an hour, until the quiche has set and is just browning.

If you can't cope with a flan without cheese, try grating a little low-fat hard cheese over the top before you put it in the oven.

Cheese

- Make good use of the low-fat hard and soft cheeses now available, e.g. Shape, Tendale, Edam, Sainsbury's 14 per cent fat Cheddar, Sainsbury's 11 per cent fat Edam, Camembert (look for the fat content on the label), Brie, Quark, Philadelphia Light.
- Cheese sauce made with flour, butter or hard margarine, milk and cheese is very high in saturated fat. An equally tasty low-fat alternative can be made, however, using skimmed milk, cornflour to thicken it and a low-fat hard cheese to flavour it. Bring out the cheesey flavour by adding $\frac{1}{2}$ tsp of Dijon mustard powder.

Sandwich fillings

All the following are low-fat sandwich fillings that are fairly moist; this means that sandwiches can be made up with the minimum (or no) low-fat spread on the bread.

- Tuna and *fromage frais*, with lettuce and finely sliced onion.
- Low-fat cottage cheese and chopped chives.
- Low-fat cottage cheese with finely chopped onions and tomato.
- Some grated low-fat hard cheese mixed with *fromage frais*; add chopped peppers (red or green), onions, tomatoes, chives, etc.
- Low-fat soft cream cheese and pickles or chutneys.
- Low-fat cottage cheese, mashed banana and a few drops of lemon juice.

- Low-fat soft cream cheese and finely chopped dried apricots.
- Low-fat *fromage frais* and reduced-sugar jam.
- Low-fat soft cream cheese and malt extract.

Low-fat soft cheeses

There is a wide range of these cheeses available now – cream cheeses, cottage cheeses, *fromage frais*, various branded cheeses. On their own they can be quite bland, but they can easily have other ingredients stirred into them to give them different flavours, for sandwiches, an accompaniment to a salad, or whatever you choose. Here are some savoury suggestions:

- Finely chopped onion
- Chives
- Fresh herbs
- Tomatoes
- Grated carrot
- Pickles
- Piccalilli
- Chutney

And some sweet offerings:

- Chopped dates
- Dried apricots
- Dried figs
- Raisins
- Marmalade
- Reduced-sugar jams
- Pure fruit spreads
- Mashed banana and a few drops of lemon juice
- Ripe soft fresh fruits

- Mashed/puréed tinned fruit in natural juice

Oat crumble topping

This is a sweet variation on the oat pastry (see page 76) which can be used with a wide variety of fruit fillings for tasty, healthy desserts.

8 oz (225 g) rolled oats
3 oz (75 g) soft brown sugar
6 tbsp soya (or peanut) oil

The ingredients should be well mixed to produce a slightly sticky (not doughy) consistency, then spread on top of the prepared fruit filling of your choice, and baked in a hot oven for 20–25 minutes. Serve warm.

Date slice

Date mixture
8 oz (225 g) stoned dates (not sugar-rolled type)
6 tbsp lemon juice

Pastry
12 oz (350 g) rolled oats
4 oz (100 g) sunflower margarine
cold water to bind

Heat the dates and the lemon juice in a saucepan, mashing the mixture with a fork. Remove from the heat and allow to cool. Make the pastry by rubbing the margarine into the oats and adding just enough cold water to form a dough. Press out half the dough on a greased baking tray, spread the cooled date mix on top, then spread the remaining pastry dough on top of the date mix. Press down firmly. Cook for 30 minutes in a hot oven.

Custard

Custard can be made with skimmed milk to reduce the saturated fat content. If the consistency is too thin for your tastes, try adding a tablespoon of dried skimmed milk powder.

Sorbets

Sorbets are a delicious and an extremely low-fat dessert – and are relatively easy to make. Here is a typical recipe:

½ pint (300 ml) water
4 oz (100 g) caster sugar
½lb (225 g) soft fruit (e.g. strawberries, raspberries, redcurrants)
1 tsp lemon juice
2 egg whites

Make up a syrup by melting the sugar and the water together over a low heat, stirring constantly. Simmer for 10 minutes, then allow to cool. Simmer the soft fruit in a little water until the fruit is soft, then rub it through a sieve. Stir the puréed soft fruit into the sugar syrup, and make up to 1 pint (600 ml) with extra water. Once cool, add the lemon juice and pour into a shallow flat container. Freeze until nearly firm.

Whisk the egg whites. Scrape the frozen mixture out of the tray and into a cooled bowl, break it up with a fork and fold in the egg whites. Return the mixture to the container and freeze until firm.

Alternatives to topping cream

A trifle made with low-fat ingredients, or even a low-fat cheesecake, can be decorated with low-fat Greek yoghurt or *fromage frais*; the former has only about 10 per cent fat, while the latter is virtually fat free. Both are thick, so hold their shape well for piping, and can be sweetened with icing or caster sugar and flavoured with a few drops of vanilla essence if desired.

Some other helpful tips

- Cut bread into thick slices when using it for toast or sandwiches. This fills you up more with the bread than with the richer filling.
- Use low-fat spreads thinly on bread/toast – you're not doing any good if you cut out butter but dollop huge quantities of low-fat spread on your toast instead.
- Try using low-fat spread on only one piece of bread in a sandwich; if it's a particularly moist filling try doing without any low-fat spread at all.
- Replace salad cream and/or mayonnaise with plain low-fat *fromage frais*.
- Whenever an egg is mentioned in a recipe, try replacing it with the whites of two eggs, and discard the yolks as they contain the majority of the fat in eggs.
- Try different brands of low-fat spreads until you find a taste that suits you.

- Some low-fat spreads look dreadful on hot toast, because of their high water content. If this is the case, simply let the toast cool before using the spread.
- Replace whole milk with semi-skimmed milk; then after four to six weeks replace the semi-skimmed milk with skimmed milk. In this way the change to skimmed milk is not such a shock to the taste buds.
- If you find skimmed milk really unpalatable, at least use semi-skimmed milk. Don't use whole milk.
- Be sure to include plenty of fresh fruit and vegetables and salad ingredients in your diet.
- If you cook your vegetables make sure you don't overcook them – they should still have some bite to them when they are served. Just steam or boil them lightly.
- High-fibre alternatives – wholemeal bread, wholemeal pasta, brown rice, cereals, etc. – all have a nuttier taste than the more refined equivalents, but the white breads, pasta and rice are good too.
- Go for white meat, e.g. veal, poultry and fish (especially oily fish), and try to avoid red meat.
- When buying red meat go for lean cuts, not cuts marbled with fat.
- Don't buy meat pies, sausages, burgers, salamis, smoked sausages, etc. They all have a high fat content.

COOKING OILS AND FATS

There are two important points to remember with
dietary fat:

- Reduce the overall amount of fat in the diet.
- Within that reduced amount of fat, the mono-
  unsaturated fats should constitute the largest proportion.

The first point is well known and most people would
accept it as common sense. The second point is a fairly
recent piece of dietary advice; until now it has been
thought that it was merely important to lower the
proportion of saturated fats and raise the proportion of
polyunsaturates and mono-unsaturates together. Manufacturers have concentrated on producing oils and
spreads high in polyunsaturates and have largely for-
gotten about the mono-unsaturates.

The table below lists the commonly available oils
and fats and indicates which category they fall into,
although it ought to be borne in mind that these are not
strict delimitations; for example, although peanut
(groundnut) oil is listed as a mono-unsaturate, it also
contains about 30 per cent polyunsaturated fats and 20
per cent saturated fats.

Manufacturers have modified their production so
that margarines and spreads high in mono-unsaturates
are now available. The best advice is therefore to:

- Cut out all the fats and oils on the list of saturates.
- Use mono-unsaturated oils in your cooking, salad
  dressings, etc., when it is feasible. This does not
  mean use mono-unsaturated oils whenever possible: merely, when a cooking oil is needed use a

small amount of mono-unsaturated oil.
- When a hard fat or spread is needed, use one that is high in mono-unsaturates or polyunsaturates.

Classification of fats and oils

Saturated	Mono-unsaturated	Polyunsaturated
Palm kernel oil	Olive oil	Sunflower oil
Coconut oil	Peanut (groundnut) oil	Safflower oil
Butter	Rapeseed oil	Corn oil
Lard	Margarines and spreads labelled high in mono-unsaturates	Soyabean oil
Hard margarine		Walnut oil
Suet		Margarines and spreads labelled high in polyunsaturates
Vegetarian suet		
Standard soft margarine		

MILK

The fat content of milk is not enormously high – 3.7 grams of fat per 100 grams of milk – but because milk is consumed in relatively large quantities, you should be aware of its fat content. For example, if you consume a pint (600 ml) of milk during the course of a day, that will contribute about 20 grams of fat to your intake, much of it saturated fat.

Cream is made by separating off the yellow fat-rich layer that floats on the top of ordinary milk – the thicker the cream, the higher the fat content. Because of this, double cream is in a class of its own as regards fat content, although single cream isn't far behind.

For these reasons it is sensible to avoid the various types of cream that are available, and to go for skimmed milk and semi-skimmed milk instead of whole milk.

- Skimmed milk has had virtually all the fat content removed.
- Semi-skimmed milk still has some fat content, but considerably less than whole milk.

Many people find skimmed milk too thin and unpalatable for everyday use, for example on their breakfast cereal or in their tea. However, it is worthy trying, perhaps after acclimatising the taste buds to semi-skimmed milk for a few weeks. In cooking, though, skimmed milk can be used with impunity; you might arrive at a compromise, in which semi-skimmed milk is used for tea, cereals, etc., and skimmed milk is used in cooking.

Goats' and sheep's milk

Goats' milk and sheep's milk are very useful alternatives to cows' milk if you have an intolerance to cows' milk. However, they should not be considered as a healthy alternative to cows' milk if you have a raised blood cholesterol level, as they both have significantly higher fat content than cows' milk; goats' milk is markedly high, at 4.8 grams of fat for every 100 grams of milk, and sheep's milk is nearly twice as fatty, with 6.9 grams of fat per 100 grams of milk. Both of these milks, and the cheeses, yoghurts, etc., made from them, should therefore be avoided if you want to lower your blood cholesterol levels.

Low-fat dairy produce

As a result of various pressures, there is now a plethora of low-fat dairy produce available. You need only look along the shelves in the local supermarket to see how big the range is:

- Low-fat butter-based yellow spreads to be used instead of butter.
- Low-fat single and double cream.
- Low-fat ice creams.
- Low-fat and very-low-fat yoghurts.
- Half-fat and low-fat soft cheeses.
- Low-fat and very-low-fat *fromage frais*, rather like yoghurt.
- Reduced-fat hard cheeses.

These are just some of the examples – if you shop around you will undoubtedly find more. The super-markets are well aware that a sizeable chunk of their market now wants low-fat products, and are bringing out new products each year.

But remember, unless something is labelled 'very low fat' or 'virtually fat free', it will still have some fat in it; for example, you can get low-fat Cheddar-type cheese, but it still contains 14 per cent by weight fat, which is quite a lot. If you are aiming to reduce your fat intake, and particularly your intake of saturated fats (which dairy produce is rich in), you should go for the very low-fat and virtually fat-free products, use the low-fat products in moderation, and try not to use the full-fat dairy produce at all.

COFFEE

Most people enjoy a cup of coffee or two during the day, although many will not touch it in the evening because they feel it keeps them awake. Furthermore, those with blood pressure problems often try to avoid coffee. Both the insomnia and the blood pressure problems appear to be caused by the caffeine found in a drink of coffee; tea (and some other drinks) also contain caffeine, but it does not appear in the drinks in such concentrations as it does in coffee. This is why decaffeinated coffee is now so popular.

However, recent research seems to indicate that there is another chemical in coffee which, if consumed excessively, can raise blood cholesterol. Details of the precise mechanism are still not clear, but you do need to drink in excess of six cups of coffee a day for the effect to be noticed, although for those who have a filter coffee machine permanently on the go in the corner of the office, this is an amount that might easily be consumed. What is of significance is that this cholesterol-raising effect occurs with both caffeinated and decaffeinated coffee.

As with so many things, it is probably best to drink coffee in moderation.

COOKING WITHOUT EGGS

If you need to reduce your dietary intake of eggs drastically, it is easy to avoid eating them on their own – boiled eggs, scrambled eggs, or whatever – but how do you make cakes without eggs? How do you make flans without eggs? At first sight, your menus are going to be a bit dull, aren't they?

- The first thing to realise is that it is the egg yolk that contains the cholesterol and saturated fats – the egg white has no cholesterol, is rich in protein and sets when heated. So one option is to use eggs but throw the yolks away. However, this is extremely wasteful, so you may want to consider other option.
- There are many cake and pudding recipes that don't call for eggs to be used. Vegetarian cookery books are a useful source of such recipes.

- In flans and quiches silken tofu can be used instead of eggs and milk
- There are at least two 'egg replacers' on the market. One is called Loprofin, and is made by Nutricia Dietary Products; the other is Ener G and is marketed by General Designs. Neither is very widely available, although can often be found in healthfood and wholefood shops. Both can be used in cooking instead of eggs – instructions are on the respective packets.

MEAT SUBSTITUTES

If you are really keen on experimenting with new foods in order to reduce your total fat intake, and in particular your saturated fat intake, you could try tofu. Not only is it low in fat, but the fats it contains are either mono-unsaturated or polyunsaturated. It is an adaptable and versatile ingredient, made from soya bean curd, and can either be used on its own, for instance as an addition to salads or stir fried with vegetables, or as an addition or as a thickener, for example in flans or cheesecakes.

Tofu can be bought in two basic forms. Silken tofu is the softest, and can easily be mashed or blended, while firm tofu is pressed hard so that it can be chopped or sliced into various recipes. Other versions of tofu, between silken and hard, can also be obtained.

Quorn is made from a mushroom-like fungus, bound with egg white. The result can be sliced, diced or shredded, and is also produced in a minced form. It has a meaty texture that absorbs the taste of foods with which it is cooked, so you can interchange it with tofu in such recipes as casseroles and curries. In its minced form it can be used in dishes that traditionally incorporate minced meat, such as lasagne and moussaka.

COOKING WITH OAT BRAN

Recently oat bran has been advocated as a dietary means of helping you to lower your cholesterol levels. As well as occurring in porridge oats, rolled oats, jumbo oats, oatmeal, it can also be bought over the counter in many healthfood shops, either loose from sacks or tubs or prepacked with a brand name on it.

Oat bran can be a valuable addition to a diet aimed at reducing your cholesterol levels (see pages 102–4). However, on its own it's pretty bland and unappetising stuff, so needs to be worked into your cooking. Here are some ideas as to how it might be used.

- Cakes
- Buns
- Biscuits, both sweet and savoury
- Bread, assuming you bake your own
- Pastry
- Porridge, added to the oats, not instead of it
- Ready-to-eat breakfast cereals
- Muesli, either bought or homemade
- Pancake batter
- Soups
- Stews and casseroles
- As a coating, e.g. for fish
- As a filler, e.g. in a meatloaf
- Homemade burgers, sausages
- Lentil loaf/roast
- Quiches/flans
- Ratatouille
- Stewed fruit
- Pies

- Crumble toppings
- Yoghurt

EATING OUT

Obviously, when you are eating out it is harder to control what you are eating, simply because you don't know what's gone into the dishes. However, as you become more aware of the foods that raise and lower your cholesterol levels, you will become more discerning in your choice of restaurants and the dishes they serve. Initially the advice might be not to eat out too often, but as you become more adept at manipulating your diet to suit your needs you can become more relaxed about eating out. Here are a few guidelines:

- Simple starters include chilled fruit juice, melon cocktail, clear soups, salads with no dressing or only a small amount of olive oil dressing.
- Main courses might include fish, poultry, lean meat, some vegetarian dishes, but try and avoid anything that has a sauce or gravy with it.
- Fresh vegetables and jacket or boiled potatoes, without sauces or butter, or, again, a salad without a dressing.
- For dessert, go for a fresh fruit salad or just fresh fruit, or a sorbet, or plain ice cream. Avoid the sundaes and confections topped with cream, sauces and chopped nuts.
- If you must eat cheese, go for the lower fat cheese such as Edam, Camembert, Brie; eat them with water biscuits if they are available, and don't use butter on the biscuits.
- Avoid cream liqueurs and so-called 'connoisseur' coffees topped with thick cream.

- If you can't drink your tea/coffee black, ask for milk – don't accept cream.

Eating out must remain a pleasure, not a nightmare. It's no fun watching your friends tucking into dishes rich with creamy sauces while you nibble a limp lettuce salad. Choose your restaurants wisely and be aware of what you're eating, and you will be able to eat as exciting meals as anyone else. And don't be afraid to ask your waiter or waitress about what goes into various dishes, how they are cooked or whether they can be served without a sauce.

7

Changing your lifestyle

During a routine well-woman medical check cholesterol lumps were noticed on my knuckles and Achilles tendons. This was a great shock to me as three such lumps had been noticed before, but had been shrugged off when I said that other members of my family also had them.

I was given a fasting blood lipid test, and my cholesterol level came out at 10.8 – very high. Next my two children were tested, Darren, eight years, and James, one year. Darren's reading was 9.0 and James was 12.8, three times higher than it ought to have been.

I have participated in sports all my life – I was then 34 and was playing league squash four times a week, and we all looked and felt very fit. So it came as a huge blow to discover we had familial hypercholesterolaemia (FH), with a high risk of heart failure.

Our diet had to be modified, but this was not too difficult as we already used polyunsaturated fats and skimmed milk. The two things which were principally banned were cheese and eggs, although over the years we have been able to eat eggs occasionally as the dietitians' thinking has changed. Unfortunately low-fat cheese is still not a good substitute for a lovely piece of Stilton or farmhouse Cheddar – these are regarded as treats or used as a main meal. None of us were great red meat eaters, so eating fish and chicken was no hardship.

Although my consultant told me to stop my sports, I nagged and nagged and after agreeing to regular ECGs to monitor heart performance I was allowed to take up road running. I now race regular half-marathons, in a reasonable time for a 40+ lady – I've just arrived back from racing in Tunis with Ron Hill, which was great fun. Both my children also participate, and I firmly believe it does them good. For me the exercise means I have a very high HDL level, which is the goody in warding off heart attacks.

All three of us are on medication, and will remain on it I suppose for the rest of our lives. My uncle died of heart disease at the age of 40, and both his sons had heart attacks in their 20s. Nowadays, though, the prognosis is better, and we all look forward to leading long happy lives.

By now it should be apparent that if you want to reduce your blood cholesterol level, and thus reduce your risk of coronary heart disease, one of the first and most important things to do is adjust your diet so that you consume less fat, and in particular less saturated fat. If you can change your diet in this way, and in a manner that does not make you feel like an outcast or a deprived member of the family, you are halfway there.

But you must always remember that the aim is not to

lower blood cholesterol levels as an end in itself. This is merely a means to an end, the aim being to lower your risks of suffering from coronary heart disease. It is a laudable aim to get your blood cholesterol levels down towards the 5.2 mmol/l mark, but it is going to be hard to do this, and the effort will be undermined if you continue to lead a life that is overloaded with other risk factors. If you want to lower your risks of coronary heart disease you need to look at *all* the risk factors in your life, and do something about each one. This means principally:

- Your weight – are you too heavy?
- Exercise – do you get enough?
- Giving up smoking.
- Alcohol – do you need to cut down?
- Stress – are there too many stresses in your daily life?

REDUCING WEIGHT

Being overweight is a risk factor for heart disease, and is often associated with high blood pressure and high blood cholesterol levels. There are all sorts of tables and charts you can use to determine whether or not you are overweight, but most people usually know whether or not they are overweight, even without weighing themselves, although whether they admit it or not is another question. Statistics show that about 45 per cent of the UK population is overweight, and 14 per cent have a serious weight problem.

If you are in the category of being seriously overweight you will probably have already received dietary advice from your GP, who should have impressed on you the dangers of being obese and made you aware of

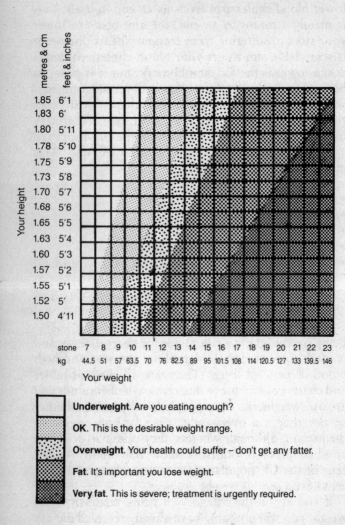

Underweight. Are you eating enough?

OK. This is the desirable weight range.

Overweight. Your health could suffer – don't get any fatter.

Fat. It's important you lose weight.

Very fat. This is severe; treatment is urgently required.

Guidelines for body weight relative to height

the limitations this obesity will already have imposed on you. For example, if you are 50 kg overweight you are having to carry around the equivalent of a sack of coal – up and down stairs, when you're doing the shopping, when you're at work. So you can imagine all the extra work your body is having to do to cope with this extra burden.

Fortunately, few of us are as much as 50 kg over-weight, but the sack of coal analogy is a useful one to work with. Say you are merely 10 kilos (1½ stone) overweight; this is equivalent to carry 10 bags of sugar around. If you are 13 kilos (about 2 stone) overweight you can think of this as about 13 bags of flour.

But how are you going to shed this extra weight – dump this shopping – that you're carting around with you? The easy answer is to eat less and to take more exercise. If you eat 2,600 kilocalories of food each day and only use up 2,500 of these kilocalories, you are going to put on weight – not rapidly, but over a period of time. Unfortunately, this is a very easy answer, and doesn't always quite tally with reality. There are those people who can stuff themselves with food and don't appear to put on weight, and others who put on weight at the whisper of a sweet wrapper; in short different people appear to have different abilities to cope with different amounts of food, and to adjust to varying amounts of food.

However, having recognised this variability in peo-ple's ability to process and burn up the food they eat, most people know, if they're honest with themselves, what they should be eating if they are to maintain themselves within a healthy weight range. And if they don't know this, they can usually work out where the extra is coming from if they keep a food diary, noting over the course of a week every bit of food they eat, right down to the last chocolate and crisp and pint of beer.

But knowing what your correct weight should be and then achieving it are two different things, and a whole industry has grown up around the latter. Here is not the place to go into a detailed rundown on precisely how to lose weight – there are as many different methods as there are days in the year – but some general guidelines may be helpful.

To begin with, if you adopt the low-fat cholesterol-lowering diet that we have already outlined, you will tend to come down towards your natural weight. Because you will be cutting out some of the fat in your diet (which is energy dense) and substituting it with complex carbohydrates (which are comparatively low in calories compared to bulk), you will automatically tend to reduce the number of calories you take in during the course of a day. Couple this with an increase in exercise (see next section), and this might be all that's needed to lose your extra weight.

If more drastic action is needed, you should always remember that once you have lost weight you need to keep it off. It is pointless losing all the weight you want on one of the very low calorie diets (VOLDs), e.g. the liquid meal replacements, if you cannot maintain this weight loss once you return to the real world. There is what is known as the rebound effect; your body seems to get used to surviving on the reduced calories of a weight-loss diet, so that when you return to normal eating your calorie intake is much in excess of what your body has got used to coping with, and you put weight back on rapidly. It is far better to lose weight slowly and steadily on a near-normal diet, taking more exercise than in the past, than to lose weight rapidly on an extreme and impractical diet.

EXERCISE

The benefits of exercise are numerous and well known – a list of such benefits could go on for pages and pages. But despite these obvious benefits, we seem more and more to be leading lives in which regular exercise plays no regular part: we all have cars, so there's no need to walk; food is comparatively cheap, so there's no need to garden and grow your own food; we all have TVs, so there's less inclination to seek out other forms of leisure activity; and we all have labour-saving machines in the house which remove much of the strenuous activity from everyday household life. For a time children seemed to be immune to this creeping effect of affluence, but even they are succumbing now – sports and games are less of a priority in the school timetable, school transport or a lift to school are taken for granted, and our roads are deemed too dangerous for kids to go cycling.

'All right', you might say, 'I can find time in a pretty busy day to take some exercise. But how is it going to reduce my risk of heart disease? What are the benefits going to be?' Well, ignoring the benefits of feeling in better health generally, it will make your heart stronger. If you take exercise, your heart has to pump more blood round to service the muscles you're using; if you take regular exercise, the heart acclimatises to this new regime and gets bigger and stronger, so that it can work more efficiently. As a result of this and other factors, any tendency to raised blood pressure is also reduced. And you also stand a fair chance of losing weight. If you look back to Chapter 3, you will see that raised blood pressure and being overweight are both additional risk factors for coronary heart disease, on top of any raised cholesterol level you might have.

But exercise also appears to have a direct effect on our blood cholesterol levels. Worry and stress seem to mobilise our stores of fat, providing readily available reserves of energy in the bloodstream should we need them. But invariably twentieth-century stress does not require us to exert ourselves in battle or in running away – we just sit there and worry some more, or drive round the corner to see the bank manager, or whatever. These mobilised reserves of fat, circulating as lipoproteins, are therefore left available to add to atherosclerotic deposits. However, if we take regular exercise these circulating lipoproteins can be taken advantage of – regular exercise in fact appears to have a direct reducing effect on the level of LDL cholesterol in the blood. There's more to it than that, though. There are various degrees of exercise, and the more ferocious the exercise the more your pulse rate will go up, i.e. your heart will beat more rapidly.

There is a formula to calculate how much exercise is needed to gain further benefits. Take the number 220 and subtract your age from it, e.g. if you are 40 the answer with be 180. Assume this to be a maximum pulse rate. If you are unfit, you should aim to exercise so that your pulse rate rises to 60 per cent of this figure, i.e. using our example of a 40-year-old, you should have a raised pulse rate of 108 beats per minute; if you are fit, this should be up to 70 per cent, i.e. 126 beats per minute.

Your pulse rate can be found easily by placing the flats of the first two fingers of your right hand on the inside of your left wrist, two finger-widths below the wrist crease. Alternatively find your neck pulse: place the same two fingers flat against the right-hand side of your neck, about three finger-widths below your chin and towards the front of your neck. Time the pulse rate

Guidelines for pulse rate after 10–20 minutes of brisk exercise

Age in years	Maximum heart rate (220 minus age) in beats per min.	Heart rate after exercise if unfit, in beats (60% of max. rate)	Heart rate after exercise if fit, in beats per min. (70% of max. rate)
15	205	123	144
20	200	120	140
25	195	117	137
30	190	114	133
35	185	111	130
40	180	108	126
45	175	105	123
50	170	102	119
55	165	99	116
60	160	96	112
65	155	93	109
70	150	90	105

over 15 seconds and multiply by 4 to give you your pulse rate per minute.

You should be aware of the changes in your pulse rate after exercise, as you will be breathing more rapidly and will probably notice your heart beating. Be careful not to overdo it, though, and do not continue if you feel any pains in your chest. It is always best to consult your doctor before embarking on a programme of strenuous exercise.

Assuming all is well, though, and you do this sort of exercise three or four times a week – a brisk mile or two's walk incorporating one stiffish hill would be enough – you should notice an effect on your HDL cholesterol level. It will be raised. And as you should have gathered by now, this is a good thing as HDL removes cholesterol from the peripheral tissues, including atherosclerotic deposits, and takes them to the liver. So:

- Regular exercise lowers LDL cholesterol levels.
- Regular brisk exercise raises HDL cholesterol levels.

And both of these are of benefit in reducing your risks of coronary heart disease.

STOP SMOKING

If some company were to arrive on the scene tomorrow with the aim of launching a new product made from the leaves of a plant that were dried, processed, shredded, treated with a load of chemicals, and then packed into thin paper tubes so the consumer could smoke them, they would probably be asked why, why would anyone want to inhale smoke when the usual reaction is to avoid smoke? 'Ah, they'll enjoy smoking them as they contain a stimulant. And once they start they won't be able to stop because they're addictive. There are one or two slight problems; for example, we have discovered that they give a huge risk of cancer of the lung. But I'm sure the public will take to them.' Fat chance – they wouldn't be allowed near the public.

Unfortunately, we're stuck with cigarettes now, and with all the health risks they confer. Note, we don't say we think there are health risks: we know very definitely there are health risks. The links between smoking and lung cancer have been well publicised. But there are also very well-documented and proven links between smoking and the risk of coronary heart disease. As was stated on page 27, someone who smokes a packet of 20 cigarettes a day is at least twice as likely to suffer from coronary heart disease, and this increased risk takes a number of years of nonsmoking to diminish to the level of the permanent nonsmoker. Furthermore, this is an independent risk factor for heart disease – it is on top of other risk factors such as raised blood cholesterol levels.

The advice is therefore to stop smoking, for a multitude of reasons. And this advice applies particularly to women. Women are protected against the risks of coronary heart disease by high levels of the female sex hormones circulating in their bloodstream before the menopause; after the menopause these sex hormones diminish, as does the protection against heart disease conferred by them. Smoking somehow seems to bring on the age of menopause earlier, so not only does smoking add its own risks as regards coronary heart disease, but for women is also appears to remove their natural protection against risk at an earlier age.

Giving up smoking is not nearly so easy as many nonsmokers might think, and for some exsmokers the craving never really disappears – smokers have been known to relapse 20, 30, even 40 years after giving it up. However, smokers must realise that it can be done – millions of smokers have become nonsmokers. It might be hard, and might need a profound change of attitude in order to gain the motivation to give up successfully, but it can be done. There are many tricks to help you on the way, many products available that are designed to make the process easier, but fundamentally you must want to give up, and often it is the process of educating yourself about the health risks attached to smoking that provides the impetus.

ALCOHOL INTAKE

Note that this section is not headed 'Reduce your alcohol intake' or 'Stop drinking'. Alcohol in itself is not a problem; indeed, some studies have shown that a glass or two (and no more) of wine a day might be instrumental in slightly raising HDL cholesterol levels, which are protective against coronary heart disease.

However, excessive alcohol consumption is a problem. It can undermine people's lives and their families' lives, it can have profound effects on health, and in particular it can be a risk factor for coronary heart disease. How much excess drinking is a risk factor for heart disease is virtually impossible to quantify, for two chief reasons.

- It is extremely rare to find alcohol abuse as a problem on its own. It is invariably associated with other problems such as smoking, obesity, raised blood pressure and raised blood cholesterol levels. The various risk factors therefore interact with each other.
- Different people have different tolerance levels for alcohol – some people get drunk more easily than others. Women, for example, have been shown to need less alcohol to become intoxicated than men. How much this affects the risk of coronary heart disease is not known though.

If you are going through the process of reviewing your diet in an effort to lower your blood cholesterol level it would be prudent to assess your alcohol intake as well. For a start, if you have a weight problem, the alcoholic drinks you consume are a rich source of completely 'empty' calories, and will certainly be contributing to the weight gain. And if you are a heavy drinker you are definitely at increased risk of coronary heart disease.

'Me? A heavy drinker? Nonsense.' Probably true. But try keeping a diary of alcohol consumption. You might be surprised at how much you get through. A couple of pints of beer a day, or two large gins at home immediately puts you over the one to two glasses of wine suggested for raising HDL cholesterol levels – it's more like the equivalent of four glasses of wine. Then what about the binges or parties at the weekend? It all adds up, and the weekly total might come as something of a shock, especially as the recommended weekly total as 21 units (i.e. the equivalent of 21 glasses of wine or $10\frac{1}{2}$ pints of beer) per week for a man and 14 units (14 glasses of wine or 7 pints of beer) for a woman. Obviously if you are slightly over this guideline you need not worry, but if your regular weekly total is two or three times this limit it is time to do something about it.

Heavy drinking is like smoking. It is difficult to give up, as the temptation is all around you, it's all pervasive. Both nicotine and alcohol are legally sanctioned addictive drugs. If anything the social pressures to drink are greater than those to smoke, with the exception of drinking and driving. However there is a slowly changing attitude, helped along by the availability of non-alcoholic beers and wines. But, like smoking, to cut down on alcohol intake if it is at problem levels requires a motivation based on a knowledge of the likely benefits. Always remember, heavy drinking increases the risk of coronary heart disease, as well as causing a number of other health problems – if you drink only moderately you will reduce these risks significantly.

STRESS REDUCTION

The topics we've covered so far in this chapter have all looked at ways you can affect directly your blood cholesterol levels or ways you can reduce the other risk factors for coronary heart disease. When we start to look at stress reduction we move away from theory and more into the area of hypothesis and speculation based on common sense.

One thing is known. If we exposed to stress, we produce two hormones, adrenaline and noradrenaline, that between them are responsible for what is known as the 'fight and flight' response. In the earlier days any stress would probably have been life threatening – an attack or a natural disaster – and this fight or flight response geared us up to do just that, stay and fight or run away as fast as possible. Today our stresses are more sophisticated and our responses have to be likewise; it is socially unacceptable to wallop the traffic warden who gives you a parking ticket, and running away would be considered most peculiar if you were asked an awkward question at a job interview.

The immediate result of this 'fight and flight' response is to increase the heart rate, increase the blood pressure by shutting down many small arteries and increase the blood lipid level. All this is fine if we fight or run, but if we don't we are left in a state of physical overexcitement that may spill over into the next stressful challenge. And one result of this unresolved stress is that the build up of atherosclerotic deposits is increased. Defusing this stress 'bomb' is therefore of importance.

Basically there are three ways to deal with stress. You can:

- try and avoid it;
- change your attitude, so that what was stressful is no longer perceived as stressful;
- learn to relax more so that you can limit the physical consequences of stress.

Avoiding stress does not mean shutting yourself away in your bedroom with your head under the pillow – that would be unrealistic. But if you find travelling to and from work in the height of the rush hour leaves you wound up and fit for nothing, see if you can arrange to travel earlier or later. If you have a personality clash with an employee or employer, see if you can change shift or change areas of responsibility so that your paths don't cross. In most cases, though, you can't remove stresses as easily as that – you have to learn to live with them and cope with them. And to do this is none too easy as it involves a change in attitude towards the stressful event, such that it is de-stressed, i.e. is no longer seen as stressful. There are many ways of doing this, but none of them are learned overnight and may as a result involve some fundamental changes in your life. For example, many of the eastern disciplines teach you these skills; yoga is one of the best known examples, and you will find yoga classes at virtually every adult education centre in the country. As well as teaching you to be more relaxed about life, yoga will also make you fitter and more in tune with and aware of your body and health. It is not a pastime merely for bored housewives: men can do it just as well as women.

Surprisingly to many of us in the west, the eastern martial arts are also a valuable path to relaxation, fitness and inner peace. Anyone who thinks judo and karate are simply about winning street brawls is labouring under a huge misconception; judo and karate have much in common with yoga, and virtually nothing in common with boxing.

Lastly, you need to learn to relax rapidly after a stressful event. To learn relaxation there are many techniques – deep breathing, muscle relaxation, meditation, to name but three – and some may be more suited to your personality than others. Try one or two, and see what effect they have on you.

All of the foregoing ignores the fact that some people seem to be inherently better at coping with stress than others – they are generally more relaxed, more easy going, don't lose their tempers, don't make a drama out of a crisis. These are characterised as type B personalities, while type A personalities tend to be more competitive and less capable of coping with stress. It has been found that type B personalities have reduced risk of coronary heart disease compared to type A personalities, although the precise statistics are hard to quantify as other risk factors invariably interfere and mask the results. It does point to the fact that more relaxed people are less at risk of coronary heart disease.

INVOLVING THE FAMILY

This is perhaps the key to the problem. If you are trying to change your diet and other aspects of your life so that your cholesterol level is brought to within healthy limits, and other risk factors for heart disease are reduced, you will find it much harder if the rest of your family continues in the ways you are trying to change yourself. What is worse is if they look upon you as some kind of weirdo or health freak, and scoff at your attempts to improve your chances of good health.

Given the UK's generally benighted attitude to good health, any individual who tries to improve their health has to expect a certain amount of derision from some people, although this attitude is mercifully on the decline. What is even more undermining is if the close family also takes this line – expecting compliance with a low-fat lipid-lowering diet will then be next to impossible.

It is imperative therefore to involve the whole family in the changes to diet and lifestyle. After all, a low-fat cholesterol-lowering diet and lifestyle is no more than a healthy diet and life – it should not and need not be perceived as onerous, bland or boring – and as such is worthwhile for each and every member of the family.

8

Dietary supplements and remedies

If you are discovered to have raised blood cholesterol levels you will undoubtedly be encouraged to change your diet and lifestyle to bring these levels down to within acceptable limits. No doctor is going to advocate any other sort of treatment until he or she is convinced that you have done all that is within your power to bring down these levels by your own efforts. But there are various remedies that are available over the counter, in various shops, that you can use as an adjunct to diet and lifestyle changes. In this chapter we will examine these non-prescription remedies to see how effective they can be and how you ought to take them. However, you must always remember that they are not to be thought of as effective on their own; they must always be considered as one part of a package of measures you should take to lower blood cholesterol levels.

There are four particular remedies that, to varying degrees of effectiveness, appear to work:

- Oat bran.
- Garlic.
- Fish oil supplements.
- Niacin.

We will then look at lecithin, which has been recommended in the past but which appears to have little basis for use.

OAT BRAN

We have already seen (in Chapter 5) how important fibre is in the diet. In particular, it was explained that soluble fibre can have a definite effect on cholesterol levels in the blood; the bile salts in the digestive tract bind to the soluble fibre and pass out of the system in the faeces, so cholesterol has to be 'diverted' into making more bile salts, therefore reducing the level of circulating cholesterol in the bloodstream.

All fruit and vegetables contain varying amounts of soluble fibre, but particularly rich sources are the legume vegetables – peas and beans – and oats. We have already talked about the importance of eating plenty of legume vegetables, especially the dried beans and pulses such as chickpeas, lentils, red kidney beans, haricot beans, soya beans, etc.; they are not only valuable sources of soluble fibre, but also of healthy starch and protein. Let's now look at oats.

Oats are a cereal, like wheat, rye or barley. However what we buy in the shops as porridge oats, jumbo oats or oatmeal are the products of quite a complex processing, in which the cereal is stabilised, steamed, dried, hulled, polished, cut and, if sold as oats as opposed to oatmeal, steamed again and flaked. Oatmeal and oat flakes are both rich in soluble fibre, and this is as good a reason as any to incorporate oats in your diet, both in the form of breakfast cereals and in pastries, crumble toppings, biscuits, cakes, etc.

But the richest source of soluble fibre – the oat bran – is removed during this processing (though breakfast cereal manufacturers are now incorporating oat bran in some of their products – see below). Most health-food and wholefood shops sell oat bran, which can easily be incorporated into various aspects of your cooking in order to increase your soluble fibre intake (see pages 86–7).

Does oat bran work to lower cholesterol levels? Studies have certainly shown that taking oat bran alone does have an appreciable effect on lowering blood cholesterol levels, but you do need to take quite large quantities of it for such an effect to make much difference – the daily recommendations vary from 50 to 100 grams (2 to 4 oz) of oat bran. You can make a creamy porridge from oat bran, which will amount to quite a sizeable proportion of the recommended amount. Alternatively, you can utilise the oat bran in your everyday cooking – adding it to ordinary porridge, for example, or to muesli, to cakes, buns, biscuits, puddings, etc. In this way you might not be able to consume the recommended 50 to 100 grams of oat bran, but you would certainly be some way towards it.

The important point to bear in mind, though, is that you would undoubtedly be using the oat bran as part of a low-fat cholesterol lowering diet, and alongside other lifestyle changes designed to complement such a diet. Eating a few grams of oat bran a day, or over the course of a week, on its own is going to have only a marginal effect of your blood cholesterol level. But if you have already switched to a low-fat diet that is particularly low in saturated fats, and which is high in other sources of soluble fibre, such as legume vegetables and fresh fruit and vegetables, adding oat bran to your cooking and breakfast cereal will give further impetus to the overall cholesterol-lowering effect of the diet.

How can you obtain oat bran? As already indicated, it is widely available in wholefood and healthfood shops, where it will be sold as bags of loose oat bran. This can then be used as you wish – some ideas for cooking with oat bran are listed in Chapter 6, while other recipes can be found in the *FHA Low-Fat Diet Book*, a companion volume to this book, by David Symes and Annette Zakary (Optima) and the *Oat Cookbook* by Mary Cadogan and Shirley Bond (Optima).

Furthermore, as the cholesterol-lowering benefits of oat bran become more widely publicised, breakfast cereal manufacturers are now producing their own breakfast cereals which incorporate oat bran. Many people find these cereals more palatable and this is a move to be welcomed, although it has to be stated that the amounts of oat bran in a typical bowl of such breakfast cereal are fairly small. So, while there are definite benefits to using these breakfast cereals, you should use them as part of a low-fat cholesterol-lowering diet.

GARLIC

Garlic has been used medicinally for thousands of years, and many properties have been attributed to it, in addition to the fact that it is one of the most important flavourings in cooking. Recently, however, studies have shown that garlic can have an effect on lowering blood cholesterol levels.

In many countries, particularly the Mediterranean countries of Europe, the consumption of garlic is a fact of life, and the aroma of garlic on the breath is taken for granted – it is not looked upon as obnoxious. This is not the case in other western countries. For this reason alone, suggesting that people consume large quantities of garlic is likely to meet with some resistance.

There is another problem, though. There appear to be a number of pharmacologically active biochemicals in garlic, but their concentrations can vary widely from clove to clove and bulb to bulb. Taking garlic medicinally can therefore be a bit of a hit or miss affair. More problematically, it can make the assessment of any therapeutic effect very difficult to quantify if you don't know what concentration of active ingredients have been employed.

To solve this problem, at least one manufacturer (Kwai) has produced garlic tablets in which the active ingredients have, as much as possible, been standardised by a process of carefully drying the garlic. As a side effect, this has kept apart the two agents responsible for garlic's pungent aroma; these agents can only come together once the tablets are exposed to the digestive process, so the odour is not apparent on the breath.

Using such tablets, it was shown that garlic does have a cholesterol-lowering effect, particularly when coupled with a cholesterol-lowering diet – the effect of the tablets (600 mg a day) plus diet was significantly greater than the effect of diet alone. Furthermore, other studies have shown that garlic can also reduce excessively high blood pressure, improve peripheral blood circulation and reduce the tendency of blood to form clots, which will have an effect on the development of atherosclerotic deposits, in addition to the lowering of blood cholesterol levels.

The advice therefore seems to be to encourage people to eat garlic – its alleged medicinal properties are many and varied, and even if only some of them are true it can only do you good. Specifically, though, garlic appears to be able to lower blood cholesterol levels, this effect being most noticeable if the garlic is combined with a low-fat cholesterol-lowering diet (and by implication a suitable lifestyle, as well). Quite large quantities of garlic, on a daily basis, appear to be needed to bring about a significant cholesterol lowering effect, and if this is required you will probably prefer to take garlic tablets. However, don't let this stop you including garlic in your diet as well.

FISH OIL SUPPLEMENTS

The interest in oily fish as a potential means of staving off coronary heart disease was aroused by the realisation that eskimos have a huge intake of fats – raw and cooked fat and flesh of seal and fish. From this one might conclude that they would suffer enormously from coronary heart disease, but in fact it is hardly a recognisable problem; so rare is it that they don't have a word for it. This is assuming they eat their traditional diet: if they move away from their traditional culture and adopt a western diet, then they get coronary heart disease the same as all other westerners.

A lot of research effort then went into trying to unravel this mystery – why did a group of people who consumed huge amounts of fatty and oily food suffer from so little coronary heart disease? And it was discovered that, although the eskimos ate a diet rich in fats and oils, these were predominantly poly-unsaturated. Furthermore, amongst these polyunsaturated fats there was one group in particular, the omega-3 or n-3 fatty acids, which occurred in relatively high concentrations and which conferred the protection against heart disease. More specifically, one of these omega-3 fatty acids, eicosapentaenoic acid (EPA), seems to be the most powerful in its effect.

But what are these effects? The first to be observed was that the blood was 'thinned' – it didn't clot so easily if the omega-3 fatty acids were present in the diet in high concentrations. This, in turn, has a direct effect on the formation of atherosclerotic deposits, as it reduces the formation of a scabby clot on top of the deposits. But there is also an earlier impact on atherosclerosis: the omega-3 fatty acids reduce the passage of cholesterol-rich blood cells into the lining of the artery wall which is thought to be the initial stage in the formation of atherosclerosis. So, it appears that the eskimos' diet does not have a specific cholesterol-lowering effect, although their cholesterol levels will be low because of the low levels of saturated fat in their diet. Of more importance to us is the fact that the omega-3 fatty acids in their diet actively limit the onset of the atherosclerosis that causes coronary heart disease.

So what can we conclude from this? First, and perhaps most obviously, a diet rich in the cold-water oily fish that the eskimos eat can only be a good thing. This will reduce your intake of saturated fatty acids, and thus help to lower your blood cholesterol level, while at the same time supplying you with omega-3 fatty acids, and specifically EPA, which limit the onset of atherosclerosis.

What are also available are fish oil capsules and

liquids which are very rich in omega-3 fatty acids and EPA, and these can be taken as a dietary supplement. These preparations will help to limit the onset of atherosclerosis, although it is important to realise that they will not lower blood cholesterol levels, and at low doses may even raise LDL cholesterol levels slightly.

NIACIN

Niacin, or nicotinic acid (the two words are interchangeable), has long been recognised as one of the B group of vitamins, vitamin B_3. As such it has been recommended, in milligram doses, in order to prevent pellagra, although if you have a healthy balanced diet you should have no problem obtaining sufficient vitamin B_3 from your food.

What we are talking about here, though, are megadoses of niacin – instead of a few milligrams you need to take grams of niacin a day to produce a noticeable impact on blood cholesterol levels; there are 1,000 milligrams in a gram (and 28 grams in an ounce), so that 2 grams is 100 times as much as 20 milligrams. But let's not get too far ahead of ourselves.

First of all, what do these gram doses of niacin do? The action is concentrated in the liver and the result is that, by various mechanisms, the production of the very low density lipoprotein (VLDL) particles is significantly reduced. If you look back to Chapter 2 you will see that these VLDL particles are precursors for, first, intermediate density lipoprotein, this IDL then giving rise to low density lipoprotein, the particle that transports cholesterol from the liver to the peripheral tissues, including any atherosclerotic deposits. In short, then, niacin acts to limit the transport of cholesterol to atherosclerotic deposits by reducing the level of LDL cholesterol in the bloodstream. Furthermore, HDL cholesterol levels rise, which promotes the removal of cholesterol from peripheral tissues and atherosclerotic deposits, and its transport back to the liver.

Various research studies have looked at the effect of niacin on blood cholesterol levels, and have shown anything from a 10 to 30 per cent reduction in levels of LDL cholesterol in the bloodstream, with or without an accompanying low-fat cholesterol-lowering diet. This is a very significant reduction, so why isn't niacin advertised widely as an over-the-counter cholesterol-lowering agent? Put simply, because of its side effects. If you take niacin in vitamin-level milligram doses there will be no side effects: however, if you take it at doses in excess of 1 gram a day it can produce an itching flush, particularly when you start to take it. The skin feels tingly, especially around the chest, back, arms and shoulders, and you may develop a redness to the skin, as if you were sunburnt. Worst cases can develop a rash, with associated headaches. To minimise these side effects, it is recommended that people taking niacin gradually build up to the full dose over three or four weeks, and that doses are divided into three each day and taken with meals – this ensures that the drug is mixed with the food and released more slowly from the gut into the bloodstream. And there are now slow-release tablets available that are specifically designed to release the drug gradually into the gut over the course of the day.

Within the medical profession there are mixed feelings about the over-the-counter use of niacin. Some doctors feel that there is little to worry about; the short-term side effects can be minimised, and after 30 years of use at these therapeutic doses there appear to be no long-term side effects. Others are much more cautious, because it is a powerful vasodilator (it dilates the blood vessels) in these therapeutic doses. It is therefore not to be recommended for unsupervised use.

The reality is that it is available over the counter, so there is nothing to stop you using it yourself. However, if you are thinking of taking these large doses of niacin, at the very least you should discuss it with your pharmacist; preferably, though, you are strongly advised to discuss it with your doctor. He will undoubtedly find out from you what you are doing about your diet and your lifestyle, and emphasise the importance of dealing with these if you want to bring down a raised cholesterol level. If you both still think that taking niacin would be a useful adjunct to what you're doing already, your doctor will then be able to supervise its use and monitor any side effects.

LECITHIN

Lecithin is in fact a group of phospholipids; with variations, it occurs in both plants and animals, the polyunsaturated plant form, obtained commercially from soya beans, being the form normally sold over the counter in healthfood shops.

If you look back to Chapter 2, and the section on the structure of the lipoprotein particles, you will see that phospholipids are important as wetting agents or 'detergents' in order to allow the fats to mix with water. And it is this property that underpinned the claimed for lecithin as a cholesterol-lowering agent, the hypothesis being that you needed a balance of phospholipid and cholesterol in order to limit the levels of cholesterol in the blood. If the cholesterol level was high, the phospholipid to cholesterol balance was out of order and this needed to be rectified by taking lecithin as a dietary supplement. Furthermore, it was felt that lecithin could limit the deposition of cholesterol in the atherosclerotic areas on the arteries by solubilising the cholesterol already there.

Unfortunately, the research evidence backing up these claims is slight and equivocal. What is often overlooked is that the body manufactures lecithin as required. Furthermore, lecithin that is ingested in the diet is broken down into its constituent sub-units by the process of digestion, so that even if you eat large amounts of dietary lecithin you actually absorb the constituent parts, not lecithin itself (or at least, very little undigested lecithin).

The conclusion is therefore that, although lecithin may have other health promoting properties, it has no ability to lower blood cholesterol levels or to reduce the risks of coronary heart disease.

SUMMARY

The first and fundamental advice is, as before, to amend your diet and lifestyle if you have raised blood cholesterol levels – if you cannot do this, any other treatment will be undermined. You can help yourself, though, by taking various over-the-counter dietary supplements; these should not be looked upon as treatments in their own right, but as a means of augmenting the effects of your cholesterol-lowering diet and lifestyle.

Of the various products available we would recommend the use of 'natural' remedies such as oat bran, garlic (including garlic pills) and fish oil supplements. Niacin, while it is available over the counter, is probably best taken under medical supervision, while the benefits of lecithin appear to be unsubstantiated.

9

What your doctor can do

If you are discovered to have raised blood cholesterol levels, you will first be investigated to make sure they are not caused by some other disease or underlying medical problems and are not a side effect of any drugs you are being prescribed. You will be advised and helped with adopting a low-fat cholesterol-lowering diet, and encouraged to make changes in your lifestyle to back up this diet. It is only after all these avenues have been explored, and you still have persistently raised blood cholesterol levels – probably a total cholesterol of over 7.5 mmol/l and an LDL cholesterol of over 5 mmol/l, or a total cholesterol of 5.2 mmol/l if you have coronary heart disease or other serious risk factors – that your doctor will suggest trying you on prescription drugs.

The only exceptions will be those people with an inherited hyperlipidaemia, whereby the raised blood cholesterol levels are caused by a fundamental inherited problem with lipid metabolism. In these cases the blood cholesterol levels are often far in excess of 7.5 mmol/l, and although a very low-fat cholesterol lowering diet and lifestyle are a must, cholesterol-lowering prescription drugs are needed in many cases, and often early on in treatment.

PRESCRIPTION DRUGS

Quite a range of drugs is available, and which drug is prescribed will depend on the individual, the cholesterol level, other problems, and the preferences of the doctor concerned. The choice is essentially between:

- Nicotinic acid derivatives.
- Isobutyric acid derivatives, known as the fibrates.
- Ion exchange resins, known as the bile acid sequestrants.
- Probucol.
- HMG CoA reductase inhibitors, known as statins.

Nicotinic acid derivatives

Nicotinic acid (niacin) was discussed in the previous chapter, where the proven cholesterol-lowering effects of daily doses of niacin in excess of 1 gram were shown. However it was also pointed out that such doses have the unpleasant side effects of flushing and rashes. Any course of treatment with nicotinic acid ought to be under the supervision of a doctor, who will be able to advise on which of the various nicotinic acid preparations to take, how to increase the dosage over three or four weeks and how to minimise the risk of side effects.

There is also, in addition to nicotinic acid/niacin preparations, a nicotinic acid derivative, acipimox (Olbetam). Side effects are less of a problem with this drug, and it may well be the drug of choice if dietary and lifestyle modifications have proved ineffective, although safety in long-term use has not been established.

Fibrates

This is a group of drugs that can reduce LDL cholesterol levels by as much as 18 per cent, while at the same time raising HDL cholesterol levels.

- Bezafibrate (Bezalip), whose primary effect is to reduce levels of triglyceride, also acts to increase the breakdown of LDL particles, thus lowering the LDL cholesterol level in the bloodstream.
- Clofibrate (Atromid) is gradually becoming obsolete. New derivatives have proved just as effective with fewer side effects.
- Fenofibrate (Lipantil) acts to lower VLDL and LDL cholesterol levels and to raise HDL levels.
- Gemfibrozil (Lopid) reduces VLDL and LDL cholesterol by decreasing the synthesis of VLDL in the liver. It will also help to raise low levels of HDL cholesterol.
- Ciprofibrate (Modalim) has recently become available in the UK, although it has been used in France for several years. It works in a similar manner to the other fibrates.

Although all the drugs in this group can be used to lower blood cholesterol levels, they are more usually used in cases of raised triglyceride levels. Long-term safety for these drugs, although not fully established, looks good.

Bile acid sequestrants

The name of this group – the bile acid sequestrants – might give you a clue as to how they work.

It has already been shown that soluble fibre in the diet – and oat bran, for example, is a rich source of soluble fibre – can bind acids in the gut. Some of these bile acids are then excreted in the faeces, and are not resorbed in the large intestine as would normally be the case. Cholesterol is therefore 'diverted' into making more bile acids, thus reducing the levels of cholesterol circulating in the bloodstream. Bile acid sequestrants work in much the same way, although more effectively, binding the bile acids and then removing them in the faeces.

There are two bile acid sequestrants widely available, cholestyramine (Questran) and colestipol (Colestid), and they are very successful when used correctly, lowering blood LDL levels by as much as 25 per cent, in addition to any impact diet and lifestyle changes might have on the blood cholesterol levels. Many patients use these drugs on a daily basis and successfully keep their cholesterol levels within reasonable limits. The drugs also have the advantage that they remain in the gut and so don't actually enter the body.

Despite these advantages, though, there are some problems. The bile acid sequestrants can interfere with the working and functioning of other prescribed drugs, so that you have to be careful to take them at completely different times to any other drugs.

The bile acid sequestrants come in little sachets, containing a gritty powder. This can be incorporated into your cooking, but the most common method of administration is to stir it vigorously into water or fruit juice so that a suspension is formed; many people make up a jug of this suspension, keep it in the fridge and pour off the requisite dose when they need it.

The long-term safety of the bile-acid sequestrants is well established. They are very much the drug of choice when treating people who have high blood cholesterol levels and who do not respond well to dietary and lifestyle modifications, and, because of their safety and efficacy, they are certainly the drug of choice for children and women of child-bearing age. However, it must be emphasised that Questran and Colestid are not prescribed instead of a cholesterol-lowering diet; they must always be used alongside such a diet.

Probucol

Probucol (Lurselle) has a poorly understood mode of action. It certainly increases the loss of bile acids in the faeces, so its effect is somewhat similar to the sequestrants. However, it is not known how this loss of bile acids from the system is accomplished. The overall result is that LDL cholesterol levels fall by as much as 15 per cent if drug treatment is associated with a low-fat cholesterol-lowering diet, although HDL cholesterol levels can also sometimes fall, which is not such a good thing.

Long-term safety of Probucol is not established. It can sometimes cause nausea and diarrhoea, and is not recommended during pregnancy and breastfeeding. Because it accumulates in fatty tissues in the body, and these stores take about three months to be cleared from the body after you stop taking the drug, probucol should be discontinued at least six months before a planned pregnancy.

HMG CoA reductase inhibitors

The full term for these drugs is 3-hydroxy-3-methyl-glutaryl co-enzyme A reductase inhibitors. Despite their name, the action of these drugs is very elegant. All cells in the body synthesise cholesterol; if the cholesterol level in the blood falls, for whatever reason, the supply of cholesterol to the cells is reduced and the cells make up the deficit, in part at least, by increasing their synthesis of cholesterol. This cellular manufacture of cholesterol is a complex process, but one of the key steps is governed by an enzyme called HMG CoA reductase. Block the action of this enzyme and you can block the manufacture of cholesterol in the cells.

Given the fact that cholesterol is such an important part of the fabric of the human body, blocking the cellular synthesis of cholesterol is not something to be aimed for, even if you have high levels of cholesterol circulating in the bloodstream. Instead, as the name implies, the HMG CoA reductase inhibitors reduce, or inhibit, the action of this enzyme, so that not so much cholesterol is produced in the cells. The cells therefore have to obtain their supplies of cholesterol from the lipoproteins circulating in the bloodstream, with the result that cholesterol levels in the blood fall. And the effects are dramatic – reductions in levels of LDL cholesterol in the bloodstream of 40 to 45 per cent have been reported.

One such drug available in the UK is simvastatin (Zocor). This is what is known as a prodrug – as administered it is ineffective, and needs to be activated in the liver (which is its site of action) before it becomes effective. Another similar drug, pravastatin (Lipostat) is also available in the UK.

These HMG CoA reductase inhibitors (statins) may well end up being the drug of the choice for people with high blood cholesterol levels that are unresponsive to any other treatment, and could well be a lifesaver to people with an inherited hypercholesterolaemia – people with FH, for example. However, offering these drugs to someone whose blood cholesterol level is very high simply because of an inappropriate diet and lifestyle, and who has no inclination to change, poses a number of prickly questions.

Someone with FH may be diagnosed in childhood or in their teens. If they are then on statins for the rest of their life it is important to know about possible long-term side effects. At the moment doctors are cautious about prescribing the statins. The drugs have only been around since the mid to late 1980s; although their impact on blood cholesterol levels is dramatic, their long-term side-effects are still unknown. The research continues. If someone starts taking the drug when they are in their 20s, what sort of side effects are likely to show up when they are in their 40s or 60s? The short answer is we don't know – the drug companies don't know and the doctors don't know, and the doctors are understandably worried about this aspect.

THE LIPID CLINIC

Many people with raised blood cholesterol levels feel very isolated. They probably know of no one else in a similar situation and, with no one else to talk to, might have difficulty putting into practice the advice their doctor has given them.

For this reason, many district general hospitals are now running their own regular lipid clinics. These clinics provide an important element in the attempt to get those with high blood cholesterol levels to change those levels themselves.

Who is sent there?

Lipid clinics are for those people with whom the GP has had little success and, more importantly, for those who have a genetic predisposition to high circulating cholesterol levels or who are already showing disease symptoms.

The people attending the clinic will thus have been referred there by their GP, or will be relatives of such people who have been referred there and who have subsequently been found to be genetically at risk.

How does the clinic work?

When you arrive at the lipid clinic the consultant will often already have the report from the laboratory giving your circulating lipid levels – cholesterol, fasting triglyceride and HDL:LDL ratio – and will have a letter from your GP giving the reasons for referral. The consultant will ask some detailed questions, not just about what you eat and the sort of exercise you take but also about other health problems and symptoms and the drugs you might be taking for them. This is to establish early on whether the high lipid levels might be caused by some other disease or problem, such as diabetes or hypothyroidism, or heavy alcohol use, or as a side effect of other drugs such as diuretics or beta blockers prescribed for high blood pressure. Most GPs will pick up such causes, but in the patient who is being treated for a number of problems it is often easy to lose track of what is the problem and what is the side effect. The consultant at the lipid clinic is able to start at the beginning and take a fresh look at everything.

The consultant will then take a careful look at your diet, and how well you are able to comply with the dietary advice you have been given already. Here the dietitian or nutritionist working at the clinic will be able to help you with any problem areas and generally guide you towards an overall pattern of eating that is more suitable for your needs.

If you are overweight you will be told to lose weight. Again, helpful advice will be given on what you might cut down on, or where the dietary problem might lie. Some careful probing by the staff at the clinic might make you aware of where the extra weight is coming from – perhaps it's that tube of mints you munch away on during the course of the day. One tube of sweets a day might not sound like much, only a few ounces aren't they? But they're undoubtedly solid sugar, and if they're surplus to your nutritional needs they're going to be laid down as fat – an ounce or so today, and an ounce or so tomorrow, and the day after that, and so on. Three hundred and sixty five tubes of sweets a year can amount to a lot of excess weight, and it might not be until you are questioned in detail about what you eat that you even think of the sweets as part of your daily food intake.

Similarly you will be questioned about the amount of exercise you take. You might feel that a walk around the park every day with the dog, and some gardening at the weekend, or the rigours of housework, or a round of golf, all constitute a healthy bout of exercise. They are all useful, it is true, but you must always remember that for any exercise to be effective it has to raise the heart rate by an appreciable amount and you have to take such exercise at least two or three times a week. Your walk round the common with the dog might be very pleasant, but if it's all flat going and it's more of a stroll than a brisk walk, you're going to have very little effect on your heart, your weight problem or your circulating cholesterol level.

One suggestion, if you do have difficulty finding the time to take any worthwhile exercise, is to try a home exercise routine. Or how about an exercise bicycle? You can then fit in 10–20 minutes hard work on the bicycle on a regular basis, perhaps before breakfast or in the evening, and you can do this come rain, come shine, while watching TV or listening to the radio. For some this might seem particularly mind numbing, pedalling nowhere in the corner of the sitting room, but for many this might fit comfortably into their lives.

If you have high levels of circulating cholesterol and you smoke, you will be told to stop. If you persist in smoking after you have been seen a few times at the clinic you may even be asked not to attend again until you have given up, as you're wasting their time. You will certainly be given every encouragement and help with giving up.

Overall, the aim of the lipid clinic is to get you to bring down your lipid levels by your own actions, and only if necessary will drugs be used to supplement these actions. All the time you will be encouraged to take responsibility for your own health, to be aware of what you're doing to yourself, and not simply to go to the clinic and then forget about it until the next visit.

For example, a week before your clinic appointment you may be asked to go to your GP so that a blood sample can be taken and sent to the labs for analysis. This means the consultant at the lipid clinic has the results in front of him when you arrive for your clinic appointment. How convenient, you might think. But there's more to it than that. By asking you to go along to your GP, you first have to make the appointment; you then have to see your GP, who will undoubtedly ask how you're getting on; and you then have to ask for the results to be sent to the clinic. This gives you a number of reminders about what you're doing, and about the fact that you are actually doing it yourself.

At the clinic the staff will give you a diet sheet, showing you what you can happily eat regularly, what you can eat occasionally, what you might be able to eat for special treats and what you must avoid. You will be asked to stick it up in the kitchen, as a constant reminder and so your whole family can get involved. If you do not cook for yourself, you will be encouraged to discuss the recommendations with whoever does the cooking, who might be asked to come into the clinic with you so that the cooking and shopping can be discussed with the person who most usually does it all.

You will get opportunities to talk to other people attending the clinic – while waiting to be seen by the consultant or in group sessions with the dietitian or nutritionist. Videos might be shown and books recommended to you. The emphasis will be on showing you that you do not suffer from an extraordinary disease but merely from a problem that can easily be controlled by changing your lifestyle slightly, just like lots of other people are doing or have done.

Once you have lowered your circulating lipids to an acceptable level, as evidenced by a couple of consecutive test results, your visits to the clinic will be reduced to maybe one a year. However, until you get to that stage you will be seen every three months or so.

A major problem is that, with no nationally funded programme to reduce CHD and lower blood lipid levels, funding for lipid clinics has to be found from scarce resources within a health district. That they function at all is often due to the commitment of a few staff who manage to squeeze the hours out of a busy timetable, and the service that they can offer to patients, GPs and the general public is often less than they would like.

The Family Heart Association offers a support service for patients, to help maintain interest and motivation between visits to the doctor or lipid clinic, and to provide extra information about diet and lifestyles designed to manage blood fats and reduce the risk of coronary heart disease.

10

To screen or not to screen

We have seen that raised cholesterol levels in the bloodstream increase the risk of coronary heart disease, and that cholesterol levels can be lowered by dietary and lifestyle changes and, if necessary, by drug treatments. The question therefore arises: Should we be checking as many people in the population as possible, finding out what their cholesterol levels are and counselling them and treating them if necessary? In this way, is it possible to lower the massive incidence of coronary heart disease in this country?

The simple answer to both questions, unfortunately, is no. Coronary heart disease, in most cases, is caused by the combined effects of a number of so-called risk factors. It is therefore necessary to look at all these risk factors, not just one in isolation, however important that one may be. All we do know is that, whatever the precise causes or risk, controlling blood cholesterol levels should always be central to the treatment and prevention of coronary heart disease.

So, how much reduction in cholesterol is necessary? Is there an ideal cholesterol level? Or, to put it in a

wider context, is there a cholesterol level above which
you are at an ever-increasing risk of coronary heart
disease and below which you are at no risk of heart
disease?

The answer again is no. Good health cannot be
measured in quantifiable units; there is a continuous
spectrum of health, and everyone can benefit from
reducing their cholesterol. But while any reduction in
blood cholesterol level is going to reduce your risk of
coronary heart disease, it is far harder to say that above
a certain blood cholesterol reading you should definitely take measures to reduce the level, and below that
reading you should not be so concerned. As we have
seen, there are a number of risk factors involved with
coronary heart disease, and these interact and affect
each other. As well as blood cholesterol levels, you also
need to look at blood pressure, blood insulin levels,
obesity, whether the individual is a smoker, and what
sort of lifestyle is followed. There is also the suspicion
that prolonged stress may be a contributory factor in
coronary heart disease, although, as it is hard to
quantify, let alone measure, stress, this is far from
certain.

Identifying the absolute risk attached to any one
factor, such as the cholesterol level in the bloodstream,
is therefore next to impossible. To be sure, guidelines
on cholesterol levels can be arrived at, but these should
always be viewed in combination with an individual's
exposure to the other risk factors for coronary heart
disease.

Another approach, perhaps, is to look at the average
blood cholesterol level across the whole population, on
the grounds that this might point the way towards an
acceptable cholesterol level to aim for. The average for
Britain is 5.8 mmol/litre. As we shall see later in this

chapter, this is generally regarded as high. Further-more, such a bald statistic conceals other facts. Because this average value is in the middle of a range of results, it should be self-evident that 50 per cent of the population have cholesterol levels that are higher than 5.8 mmol/litre, and that a substantial proportion of the population have results that are considerably higher than they ought to be.

So, if we want to make an impact on the levels of coronary heart disease prevalent in this country, what must we do? The first piece of advice that has become abundantly clear over the years is that *everyone* can benefit from a lowering of their blood cholesterol level. Any lowering of your blood cholesterol level will reduce your risk of suffering from coronary heart disease. If other risk factors are present – family history

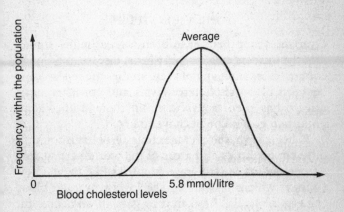

The average blood cholesterol level for the UK population is 5.8 mmol/l. As can be seen from this diagram, many people within the population have blood cholesterol levels that are considerably higher than 5.8 mmol/l.

of heart disease, middle age if a man, post-menopausal if a woman, high blood pressure, obesity, diabetes, a sedentary lifestyle – then there is an even greater imperative to adopt a lipid-lowering lifestyle, as well as tackling these other risk factors where possible.

Doctors do often check their patients' blood cholesterol levels, as well as monitoring their weight and blood pressure and other risk factors. With some patients they may decide that a change of lifestyle is all that is necessary to reduce the risk of coronary heart disease – take more exercise, eat less fat, or just eat less. With others the advice may be backed up with some form of treatment. The aim will always be to get the total cholesterol level as low as possible, and preferably below 5.2 mmol/litre, the LDL level below 4.1 mmol/litre and the HDL level above 1 mmol/litre. But how have these figures been arrived at?

POPULATION STUDIES

Over the years there have been a great many studies into the incidence of coronary heart disease in different countries, and in many of these studies the relationship between blood cholesterol levels and coronary heart disease has been analysed. From these studies some important general points have emerged.

To begin with, the average cholesterol levels found in different countries and areas of the world vary widely. At one end of the scale are countries like Papua-New Guinea, which has one of the lowest average blood cholesterol levels. As countries gain in affluence, the average cholesterol levels in the population tend to rise too. Exceptions can be seen in the Mediterranean countries, which seem to have lower cholesterol levels than might be expected. However the affluent westernised countries such as the US, Australia and the northern European countries all have the highest average blood cholesterol levels, with the UK coming out near the very top of the table. The main exception to this premise linking affluence to blood cholesterol levels is Japan; Japan is one of the most affluent countries, yet the population as a whole has a low average cholesterol level.

In line with what has already been said it should come as no surprise to discover that those countries with very low average blood cholesterol levels have very low coronary heart disease rates, Japan being one such example, while those countries with the highest average blood cholesterol levels have the highest rates of coronary heart disease, the UK being a good example of the latter. Indeed, some studies have gone so far as to suggest that the average blood cholesterol in a country is the best way of predicting the coronary heart disease rate in that country, despite the fact that there are a host of other risk factors to take into account; the thinking being that the other risk factors only begin to gain importance once the cholesterol level in a population has already put that population at risk.

There have been even more studies on groups of people within different countries, i.e. taking just one group of people and studying them over a period of years to see what happens to them. And, to a greater or lesser extent, these studies all confirm that blood cholesterol levels are linked to coronary heart disease rates – the higher the blood cholesterol level, the greater the risk of suffering from coronary heart disease.

There have also been many other detailed studies that have shown that the consumption of saturated fat in particular has a direct influence on the level of cholesterol circulating in the bloodstream – the more saturated fat you consume the higher is likely to be your blood cholesterol level. (This was looked at in more detail in Chapter 5.) But some of these population studies have also underlined this point. For example, it has already been explained that Japan has one of the lowest rates of coronary heart disease in the world and also one of the lowest average blood cholesterol levels in its population as a whole. It is believed that this is due to the diet they traditionally consume, which is very low in animal meat, particularly fatty meat, is very high in fish meat and is also very high in raw and quickly cooked vegetables. Such a diet is very low in saturated fats (and high in fish oils, which are now generally recognised to protect against heart disease). However if a native of Japan moves to, say, the US and adopts the culture and style of nutrition of the US, their cholesterol level tends to move into the range normally found in the US and their risk of coronary heart disease increases accordingly.

As a result of these findings a number of studies have been set up to see what happens if cholesterol levels are lowered within a community. Does the risk of coronary heart disease come down in parallel with the cholesterol levels?

In short, yes it does. Some studies have looked at the effect that modifications to diet have on cholesterol levels, others have looked at the effect that drugs have had on cholesterol levels, and others have tried both approaches. The results in terms of lowered cholesterol levels have been varied, but of more importance is the fact that lowering cholesterol levels has a definite impact on the incidence of coronary heart disease. Being even more specific, if cholesterol levels are lowered in middle-aged men, aged 40 to 60 – the ages at which men have the greatest increase in risk of heart disease – the impact on this risk is greatest.

These are all very bald statements, based on the results of a number of studies. Not all the studies were as conclusive as others, and point up the problems attached to carrying out this sort of research. One of the largest of these research projects was the US Multiple Risk Factor Intervention Trial, abbreviated to MR FIT; this involved studying a high risk group of men who either received what was called 'special intervention', to try and reduce their high cholesterol, high blood pressure and smoking, or received merely, what was termed 'usual care'. The trial ran for seven years, and in the end demonstrated ... nothing. No significant difference could be detected between the onset of coronary heart disease in the two groups. The most plausible explanation for this result was that the 'usual care' group had coincidentally benefited from a greater public awareness of what the risk factors are for heart disease and a willingness to do something to reduce them – deaths from heart disease at this time were falling right across the age range in the States. But it does demonstrate that trying to show cause and effect in the incidence of coronary heart disease is extremely complex.

However, we must not let the MR FIT study undermine the results that have come in from numerous other studies around the world, all of which do point to the fact that blood cholesterol levels are closely linked to the risk of coronary heart disease, and if blood cholesterol levels can be lowered in a community, the incidence of coronary heart disease also reduces. But is it possible for blood cholesterol levels to be lowered too much? Is there a point below which you endanger your health by not having enough cholesterol in your bloodstream, bearing in mind that cholesterol is an essential constituent of the human body? At one point there did appear to be evidence that too low a blood cholesterol level increased the risk of death from other causes, principally from cancer. But it is now clear that such deaths tended to occur early on in such studies, the conclusion being that the low cholesterol levels were in fact either caused by, or were incidental to, undetected but pre-existing cancers – another case of confusing cause and effect. Furthermore, if we look at countries where there is a very low average blood cholesterol level within the population we find that there is a concomitant low incidence of coronary heart disease, but no concomitant increased incidence of cancer.

LEVELS TO AIM FOR

As should be apparent by now, there is no ideal figure for blood cholesterol levels – the general rule is that the lower the blood cholesterol level the better. However, after much discussion amongst the medical profession in many countries, the following guidelines have been generally agreed on. There will be some discrepancies from country to country, but these are the guidelines that operate in the UK, and they are broadly similar to those operating in the US.

- The target range is given as below 5.2 mmol/l.
- Between 5.2 and 6.5 mmol/l there is deemed to be a mild problem; weight reduction will be advised, if necessary, and the adoption of a lipid-lowering diet. Drugs might be necessary in a very few patients.

- Between 6.5 and 7.8 mmol/l there is deemed to be a moderate problem; weight reduction will be encouraged, if necessary, as will a lipid-lowering diet; coincident risk factors (e.g. smoking) will also be controlled as much as possible, and any underlying causes of the problem will be dealt with if necessary. Drugs might be necessary if diet doesn't work.
- Over 7.8 mmol/l there is deemed to be a severe problem; weight reduction will be encouraged, along with a lipid-reducing diet; drugs may well be necessary, coincident risk factors will be controlled, and underlying causes treated if possible.

If this rationale is followed it is obvious that there will be a stepped response on the part of the doctor, depending on what the cholesterol level is; it is not an all-or-nothing response.

What is essential to remember is that this should not be an inflexible response. It has to take a lot of other matters into account – other risk factors, for example. Somebody with a cholesterol level of 6.5 mmol/l who is fat, who smokes, who takes no exercise and who has high blood pressure is going to elicit more concern from the doctor than a lean fit nonsmoker with no blood pressure problems who also has a cholesterol level of 6.5 mmol/l.

Then there is also the breakdown of the total cholesterol figure into HDL and LDL. If someone has a total cholesterol level of 6.5 mmol/l, but has an HDL of 2.2 mmol/l there is likely to be less concern than for someone with a lower total cholesterol of 6.0 mmol/l but with an HDL of only 0.9 mmol/l. Certainly, if anyone is found to have a total cholesterol level of 6.5 mmol/l or over, it is advised that they have a cholesterol test that shows both the LDL and HDL figures, and thus the LDL:HDL ratio, as well as the total cholesterol, and preferably that gives the fasting triglyceride value as well.

MEASURING CHOLESTEROL LEVELS

Blood cholesterol levels can be measured in two ways:

- Laboratory analysis.
- Dry chemistry analysers.

Of the two methods, laboratory analysis is the more reliable, but it may take a few days before the results come back to the doctor's clinic. A blood sample has to be taken from a person's vein by a doctor or a nurse; the sample then has to be sent off to the laboratory for analysis; and the results are therefore not available for a few days. Furthermore, if a full lipid analysis is required the person has to have fasted for 12 hours before the blood sample is taken; however, this means that the analysis can then yield results not only for total cholesterol but also the triglycerides, LDL and HDL.

In contrast, the dry chemistry analysers, such as the Reflotron, are marketed as a convenient means of obtaining blood cholesterol measurements instantly. Rather than requiring a blood sample drawn from a vein, a sample is taken by merely pricking a finger, a task which can be performed by anyone with the requisite training. The blood obtained is then placed on a suitable reagent strip, the strip is inserted into the machine, and a reading of total blood cholesterol is available after 3 minutes.

The dry chemistry analysers are not cheap, although smaller, more competitively priced versions are being

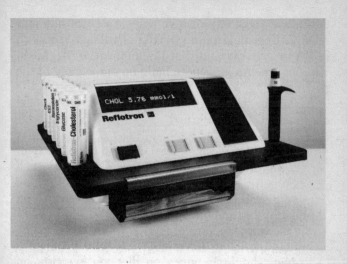

A typical dry chemistry analyser used for testing blood cholesterol

developed. Of more importance is the fact that they need to be carefully standardised and calibrated if they are to give accurate and reproducible results, and the fact that the operator needs to be skilled in taking the sample – if they are not, a false result may be obtained. There may, therefore, be variations in the accuracy of the results from machine to machine, depending on how well they have been set up, and from operator to operator.

Therefore, despite the delay in getting the result, it is recommended that screening for high coronary heart disease risk should be carried out by a doctor or nurse, should include a blood cholesterol and blood pressure test, should include a medical examination for clinical signs of familial hyperlipidaemia, and analysis of both family and personal medical records. The diagnosis, either way, high risk or low, will then be certain and reliable. If medical treatment or counselling is required, it can be given instantly, at the moment of diagnosis, without time for anxiety to build up in the mind of the patient.

As far as the interpretation of the results of the cholesterol test is concerned:

- If the total cholesterol level is found to be less than 5.2 mmol/l, and providing other risk factors such as obesity, high blood pressure, smoking, etc., are not a problem, then advice will be centred on healthy diet and lifestyle.

- If the total cholesterol level is found to be in the range of 5.2 to 6.5 mmol/l – a mild problem – advice should be given on diet, on exercise, on weight reduction if necessary, and if other risk factors, such as high blood pressure, are present, these should be addressed. There may be a follow-up check after 6 to 12 months.

- If the total cholesterol level is found to be over 6.5 mmol/l – a moderate or severe problem – more rigorous treatment will be prescribed, especially if other risk factors are present. However, consideration of the HDL, LDL and triglyceride profile will have to be given before any firm decisions on treatment are made.

SCREENING

Deciding the correct form of coronary heart disease risk analysis is one thing. Deciding who to test is quite another. In short, what sort of screening programme should we have? Put simply, there can be four sorts of screening programme:

- Mass screening.
- Opportunistic screening.
- Selective screening.
- Selective prioritised screening.

All these screening programmes cost money. If the incidence of coronary heart disease can be lowered as a result of any such screening, it will obviously save the health service, and ultimately the country, a considerable amount of money. However, this will be money saved at some indeterminate time in the future: screening costs money now.

Mass screening

In theory the only way to track down all those people with high blood cholesterol levels is to implement a policy of mass screening, in which everyone is offered the opportunity of a blood cholesterol test, and blood cholesterol testing is taken out into the community as much as possible, e.g. in special caravans or trailers situated where the public tend to congregate.

This is a path down which some countries have gone, the US being a good example. However, even in the US there is a rethink in progress, and a decrease in mass screening. Certainly mass screening does have its problems. For a start, it is expensive, and it gets increasingly expensive to reach those who have not been (or don't want to be) screened. The risk assessment is not always reliable. The analytical machines used to measure cholesterol levels need to be operated by trained staff; if such staff are not available in the large numbers needed for mass screening, then you run the risk of false positives, where people are treated who have no problem, and, even worse, false negatives, where people who do have a problem are left untreated, both arising from inaccurate results.

Furthermore, it is not enough to look only at cholesterol. Coronary heart disease risk analysis needs to consider, as well as blood pressure, body weight, diabetes in the family, personal medical record, family medical history and clinical signs. This service can only be provided by a fully trained health professional.

For mass screening to be successful you also need enough health workers who are trained in the correct interpretation of results and who can implement the correct treatment regime. Bear in mind that for many with high blood cholesterol levels they will need a combination of advice on diet, lifestyle and exercise, perhaps coupled with treatment for other disorders, perhaps drug therapy for the high cholesterol levels, and proper follow-up and monitoring. This certainly cannot be offered in a cholesterol screening trailer parked in a shopping mall in downtown Wichita Falls, Texas.

It appears that, after trying to implement a policy of mass screening in the States, the authorities are now easing off to a position of selective screening, because of the problems outlined above. In the UK we are at the other end of the spectrum – doctors in the UK have opted for a policy of selective screening, with some backing from government for preventative initiatives.

Opportunistic screening

Opportunistic screening is exactly what it says it is – screening is offered to anyone, irrespective of age, sex, other risk factors, etc. For example, anyone attending a general practitioner's surgery is offered a blood cholesterol test, whatever their reasons for going to see the doctor in the first place. The screening would not take place there and then, but at specified screening sessions, the people attending the surgery or health centre being given letters inviting them to the next screening sessions; husbands would be invited to bring wives along and, more importantly, wives would be invited to bring husbands along. Although it may be feasible to screen all age groups, it might be sensible to limit the service to those in the at-risk 40–60 age group.

Selective screening

The principle behind selective screening is that you select who you are going to screen, i.e. if resources – money, people, equipment, time – are scarce you decide who is most likely to have raised coronary heart disease risk and who is most at risk, and you then aim to test all these people.

We have already dealt with many of these issues in Chapter 4, where we saw that the principal indicators of raised coronary heart disease risk are:

* A family history of coronary heart disease or of familial hyperlipidaemia.
* A high blood cholesterol level.
* High blood pressure.
* Diabetes.
* Being overweight.
* Physical signs of primary hyperlipidaemia – xanthomas, xanthelasmas and corneal arcus.

To this list might be added smoking, as this is a high risk factor for coronary heart disease in itself.

Having drawn up a list of such indicators, the

decision then has to be made as to whether you are going to screen all people with these characteristics or not. In practice it has been shown that it is best to narrow the choice down to those between the ages of 25 and 60, and perhaps even 40 and 60. Below the age of 25 many of the symptoms of the inherited hyperlipidaemias may not have become apparent, and anyhow few people this young will think of the idea of such screening as being relevant to them. There will therefore tend to be a poor response to any request to attend for screening, and poor compliance with any advice. With people over the age of 60 the emphasis on risks other than high cholesterol become more important, high blood pressure being the prime example.

Women should be screened as well as men, but for slightly different reasons. Women do suffer from high blood cholesterol levels, but less so than men, and they have a lower incidence of coronary heart disease, at least before the age of menopause. It is important that women at high risk of coronary heart disease are identified, but perhaps of equal importance is the fact that women still do the majority of the cooking, shopping and caring. If they attend for blood cholesterol screening they can be advised generally on the importance of diet and exercise, and in this way may be able to influence the whole family. Here the line between screening and health education becomes blurred.

In terms of age and sex, the key groups are men between the ages of 40 and 60 and, to a slightly lesser extent, women between the ages of 50 and 60 – if no one else can be selectively screened, these groups should be as they show the greatest risk of coronary heart disease.

So, you are going to screen (ascertain the risk of coronary heart disease) those between the ages of 40 and 60 who also have the characteristics listed at the beginning of this section, i.e. who have a strong chance of an increased risk of coronary heart disease because of other risk factors. And in most countries, and certainly in the UK, this sort of screening is best centred on the services offered by general practitioners, as they are most likely to have the health records of the general population. Such screening would obviously be done on a voluntary basis, with letters being sent out inviting people to screening checks. People in the target group can also be screened when they attend the health centre or GP's practice for other reasons. A cheaper, and perhaps more practical alternative, is to invite people to specific screening sessions when they attend the general practice or health centre for other reasons.

Who actually operates such screening sessions will depend to a certain extent on the size and resources of the practice. Ideally, it would be sensible for a suitably trained nurse to run such sessions, and to refer patients to the doctors only if they fall outside certain limits. Most health districts in the UK now have lipid clinics based in the large district general hospitals, and they are often keen to help general practices and health centres set up such screening services.

Selective prioritised screening

In 1993 the UK government announced its Health of the Nation initiative, intended to prevent the illnesses of major public health importance, including coronary heart disease. Health of the Nation addresses information to the population as a whole on how to reduce coronary heart disease risk – healthy eating, physical activity, giving up smoking and maintaining a reasonable body weight.

This is no quick fix. Everyone agrees, including the government, that this is a long term strategy that may take 10 to 20 years, even several generations, to be effective. There is also the concern that healthy diet and lifestyle information may be taken up more by those who least need it, the people who are already fairly fit and well. We shall see.

But Health of the Nation does not only rely on individuals modifying their behaviour. It also urges corporate action to make the healthy options both easy and cheap. Furthermore, the concept has arisen of 'healthy cities', which might ban smoking in public places, serve regular healthy menus in works' and schools' canteens, and provide ample sports and fitness facilities for adults and children.

Laudable though the aims of Health of the Nation are, the initiative does tend to neglect the plight of the many people living on the brink of disaster, those at high risk of premature coronary heart disease who could die in their 50s, their 40s or even in their 30s if nothing is done to seek them out and help them. These high risk individuals may need more rigorous advice on diet and lifestyle than is appropriate for the population as a whole, and they may also need medical treatment.

The medical profession would like to seek out and help these high risk individuals. But this takes time and costs money. There is some financial provision within the NHS to screen patients for preventable illnesses. In the long term prevention is cheaper than treatment once the illness is established, while the saving in human misery is incalculable. Prevention is still in its infancy: it will develop.

One of the problems in screening for coronary heart

disease risk is the huge number of people who need to be screened and counselled. There needs to be some method of according priorities. The method favoured by the medical professions is selective prioritised screening – selecting and giving priority to people perceived from their medical records to be at risk. In this way, a higher proportion of those offered full screening would be expected to be found to be in need of immediate care.

Should you ask your doctor to screen you for high coronary heart disease (CHD) risk? Here are some of the indications that might encourage you to do just that.

- A personal history of CHD (angina, heart attack).
- A family history of premature CHD, e.g. angina, or heart attack in a blood relative younger than 60 years.
- Familial hypercholesterolaemia in the family.
- Diabetes in the family.
- High blood pressure in the family.
- Chest pains or excess breathlessness during exercise.

PUBLIC HEALTH EDUCATION

It may be that, reading this chapter, you conclude that if we were to screen the population of the UK in some way and treat those that were found to be suffering from high cholesterol levels, the epidemic of coronary heart disease that we are engulfed in would abate. Would that disease prevention were so simple. It would be like stopping a leaking boat from sinking merely by baling out the water. It's all right as a short term measure – crisis management – but it does nothing to address the fundamental problem.

And what is the fundamental problem as regards coronary heart disease? Very basically, that we in the western industrialised countries live a fundamentally unhealthy life. We eat too much, and we certainly eat too much fatty food, particularly food rich in saturated fat; we take too little exercise; we smoke cigarettes; we probably drink too much; and we are buffeted by stresses which we don't seem to be able to cope with very well.

The last problem is something we probably can't do much about, apart from to learn various methods of coping with stress and promoting relaxation. But all the other problems can be removed or reduced – all it requires to rectify these problems is a conscious decision and a will to implement such a decision. But such decisions and their implementation are dependent on some degree of motivation on the part of the individual – he or she has to know that there will be a trade-off in terms of good health. And to get this message across to the general population requires public health education. Those that have visited the States and Australia might think that many people there are obsessed with their cholesterol levels, their diet and exercise, but you can't accuse them of being unaware of the risk factors for heart disease and of what they as individuals can do to reduce these risks.

In this country, in contrast, there is less awareness of how individuals can modify their diet to lower their risks of coronary heart disease. In schools, for example, health education is limited and does not deal adequately with the effect of diet on health. And any benefit that such health education might have is sometimes undermined by the schools meals service. This is an undoubted anomaly in a country that has such a high incidence of coronary heart disease.

But public education shouldn't merely be confined to schools and children. Despite massive media coverage of the links between diet, exercise and heart disease, the general public, particularly the at-risk section of the general public, have only a poor understanding of these links. Efforts must be made to target the message more accurately. For example, parents must be made aware of the fact that a healthy diet and plenty of exercise in childhood and adolescence will reduce the subsequent risk of CHD later in life. If parents can be persuaded to change their lifestyle – diet, exercise, etc. – their children will grow up taking these changes for granted.

SUMMARY

Amongst those that are concerned with heart disease and its prevention, there is currently much debate about the advantages and disadvantages of screening and public education. Some say that screening is a net with a very big mesh, and many people slip through. Others say that public education is a blunt tool and is relatively ineffective given the sums of money that have to be spent on it. Both accusations are probably true in part, but there is no need because of that to throw either approach away completely – each can complement the other.

Perhaps a high-risk approach would be more effective, concentrating on finding and treating those already with a problem, rather than relying on adjustments to the habits of the nation as a whole.

If, as seems to be the case, resources are scarce, it would surely make most sense to target both the screening and the public health education at specific sections of the population. If we cannot afford – or it is impractical – to mass-screen the whole population, then adopt a policy of selective screening, whereby those in proven at-risk groups and those most likely to have raised cholesterol levels are screened and then counselled, advised and, if necessary, treated to lower their risk factors. If we cannot afford a policy of health education across the whole population, then target that education at specific sectors of the population. The groups with the highest risk are men and women aged 40–60, generally speaking. It might be that these groups are difficult to target successfully with a general health education programme, or they might be resistant to such messages. However, it has been clearly demonstrated that those at high risk of coronary heart disease do benefit from intervention. Perhaps, therefore, we would do better advising them on the benefits of screening to pick up the high-risk individuals. And perhaps we should also be placing more effort on educating for the future – targeting the public health education message at parents, and particularly the women, who still do the majority of the cooking and the caring, and at children.

One thing is clear, though. The UK has one of the highest incidences of coronary heart disease, and this can be reduced if the risk factors can be reduced. However, this reduction in risk factors can only be achieved if there is the will, both in the population as a whole and in those detected as being already at high risk.

11

Conclusion

At the end of the day, we must never lose sight of the fact that high blood cholesterol levels are a risk factor for coronary heart disease. It is the west's epidemic of heart disease that must be tackled, and lowering blood cholesterol levels in the individual and in the population as a whole is merely a means to this end.

The message running through this book – and it is a message that will be repeated by any doctor who sees a patient with raised blood cholesterol levels – is that treating cholesterol levels in isolation is of very little use unless the individual is prepared to do something about all the risk factors for coronary heart disease. Unless that person is unfortunate enough to be suffering from one of the inherited familial hyperlipidaemias such as FH, any high blood cholesterol level they may have is probably caused by a high fat, high saturated fat diet and too little exercise. Addressing these two problem areas will undoubtedly do much to bring down their cholesterol level to reasonable limits. But they need to be made aware of why they are trying to bring down their cholesterol level, and once they have had this link with coronary heart disease explained to them they need to look at the rest of their lifestyle and adjust it to reduce other risk factors.

Of even more benefit to the country as a whole is a nationally coordinated policy of health education and selective screening. Health education ensures that the public at large is aware of risk factors for heart disease and is encouraged to limit these factors; and selective screening ensures that those who do have high cholesterol levels or who are otherwise at high risk of coronary heart disease are identified and action taken to treat them. In this way the problem is attacked from both directions, and we will then be able to see some abatement in the UK's dreadful epidemic of coronary heart disease.

In individual terms, the message is that *you* can do something about your chances of a long and healthy life; the means are in your hands and with the knowledge you now have, you can start – today – to make the changes to your diet and lifestyle to ensure you don't become just another statistic in the UK's heart disease record.

- Do not smoke.
- Live an active life.
- Maintain a reasonable body weight.
- Eat plenty of vegetables, cereal foods and fruit.
- Go easy on the fat, alcohol, salt and sugar.
- Learn to unwind.

And if you join the Family Heart Association you will have access to information that will help you to do just that.

Glossary

adrenaline A hormone released by the adrenal glands which prepares the body for danger or stress. Amongst other things it raises blood pressure and stimulates the heart.

amino acids The basic building blocks of proteins. Human proteins consist of about 22 different amino acids, of which nine must be provided in the diet.

angina In full it is known as angina pectoris. It is an acute pain caused by lack of oxygen supplied to the heart muscle; this lack of oxygen is in turn caused by atherosclerosis.

aorta The aorta or dorsal aorta is the largest artery leaving the heart. It arches up and back from the top of the heart and descends through the abdominal cavity. It is 2–3 cm in diameter.

apolipoproteins Wetting agents that are involved in the structure of the cholesterol-containing lipoproteins. There are many different apolipoproteins, and their identification has helped isolate different lipoproteins.

arteries The blood vessels that carry blood from the heart to the peripheral tissues.

atherosclerosis The thickening and hardening of the artery walls with deposits that largely consist of cholesterol. These deposits fur up the arteries and can eventually block them.

beta blockers A group of drugs used to treat high blood pressure. Some drugs within this group can also cause raised cholesterol levels.

bile Produced by the liver, it is stored in the gall-bladder and released into the small intestine to aid digestion of fats.

bile acid sequestrants A group of drugs used to treat high cholesterol levels. They bind bile salts in the gut, preventing them from being resorbed into the body, so that cholesterol has to be broken down to make more bile salts.

bile salts The active constituents of bile, they assist in the digestion of fats by forming an emulsion of tiny fat particles.

carbohydrate A class of foods consisting largely of carbon, hydrogen and oxygen. The sugary and starchy foods that are broken down into the simple sugars by the process of digestion.

cell The basic unit of nature – all organisms consist of cells. It is the smallest part of unit of the body that can carry on independent life.

cell membrane Animal cells are bounded by the cell membrane, a complex structure which consists in part of cholesterol.

CHD Coronary heart disease.

chylomicron One of the lipoproteins that transport cholesterol in the bloodstream. In principle the chylomicrons transport cholesterol from the gut to the liver.

chylomicron remnant As the chylomicron travels from the gut to the liver it releases fatty acids. When it gets to the liver it is therefore rich in cholesterol and is known as a chylomicron remnant.

complex carbohydrate Large food molecules consisting of starch and dietary fibre.

corneal arcus The whitish-yellow ring of cholesterol

deposited around the outer edge of the iris of the eye in people with high cholesterol levels.

coronary arteries The arteries supplying blood to the heart. They are the first arteries to branch off the aorta.

coronary heart disease Disease caused by furring-up of the coronary arteries with atherosclerotic deposits. Symptoms include breathlessness, angina and heart attacks.

diabetes Disease in which the blood glucose concentration is above normal. Type I, insulin-dependent (IDDM), diabetes involves a lack of insulin; type II, non-insulin-dependent (NIDDM), diabetes involves insulin acting inefficiently.

diastole The relaxed phase of the heart's pumping cycle.

diastolic pressure Blood pressure during diastole.

eicosapentaenoic acid An omega-3 polyunsaturated fatty acid found in oily fish. It makes the blood less likely to clot and lowers the levels of LDL cholesterol, among other things.

enzymes Proteins that are essential for biochemical changes to occur. Each biochemical reaction is promoted by a different enzyme; if you destroy or limit the enzyme the reaction is limited or halted.

EPA Eicosapentaenoic acid.

essential amino acids The nine amino acids that cannot be synthesised in the human body but that are needed for protein structure. They therefore have to be provided in the diet.

essential fatty acids The fatty acids that cannot be synthesised in the human body but that are essential for everyday body functioning and structure. They therefore have to be provided in the diet.

familial combined hyperlipidaemia One of the commonest inherited disorder of lipoprotein metabolism, characterised by raised cholesterol and triglyceride levels.

familial hypercholesterolaemia One of the inherited disorders of lipoprotein metabolism, characterised by very high blood cholesterol levels.

fatty streak A layer of fat-filled cells in the artery wall. It is taken to be an early stage in the development of atherosclerosis.

FCH Familial combined hyperlipidaemia.

FH Familial hypercholesterolaemia.

fibre Indigestible plant residues that are not broken down by the process of digestion. They add bulk and roughage to the food mass in the gut.

fibrates A group of drugs used to treat raised blood cholesterol levels, although they are more used to treat raised triglyceride levels.

glycerol The backbone or skeleton of the triglyceride molecule that is the basic structure of fats and oils.

HDL High density lipoprotein.

heart attack The degeneration of part of the heart-muscle, so that it stops working. The damage is caused by furred-up coronary arteries not supplying enough oxygen to the heart muscle.

high density lipoprotein Put simply, lipoprotein that transports cholesterol from the peripheral tissues to the liver. It appears to remove cholesterol from athero-sclerotic deposits.

HMG CoA 3-hydroxy-3-methyl-glutaryl coenzyme A.

HMG CoA reductase The enzyme responsible for the conversion of HMG CoA to mevalonic acid, a key stage in the synthesis of cholesterol in the body's cells.

HMG CoA reductase inhibitors A group of drugs that block HMG CoA reductase and thus limit the synthesis of cholesterol in the body.

hydrogenated fats Unsaturated fats (from plants) that have been saturated (hydrogenated).

hypercholesterolaemia Raised blood cholesterol levels.

hyperlipidaemia Raised blood lipid levels, i.e. raised levels of cholesterol, triglycerides, or both.

hypertension Raised blood pressure.

hypotension Low blood pressure.

hypothyroidism Low production of thyroid hormone. One side effect is to raise blood cholesterol levels.

IDL Intermediate density lipoprotein.

infarct Death of an area of tissue, e.g. muscle.

insoluble fibre Dietary fibre that is relatively inert and incapable of absorbing water and other compounds in the gut, e.g. wheatbran, lignin.

intermediate density lipoprotein An intermediate stage in the production of cholesterol-rich low density lipoprotein.

ion exchange resins Drugs used as bile acid sequestrants in the treatment of raised cholesterol levels.

isobutyric acid derivatives Fibrate group of drugs.

LDL Low density lipoprotein.

lipids A group name for fats and oils, lipoproteins, phospholipids and cholesterol.

lipoprotein A particle in which fats are transported in the bloodstream. A lipoprotein particle consists of varying proportions of triglycerides, cholesterol, phospholipids and apolipoproteins.

low density lipoprotein Put simply, lipoprotein that transports cholesterol from the liver to the peripheral tissues, including to atherosclerotic deposits.

marine triglycerides Oils extracted from cold-water oily fish. These oils are rich in omega-3 fatty acids, particularly EPA, and are an effective over-the-counter treatment to limit the onset of atherosclerosis.

mass screening A policy by which everyone in the

general public is checked for a particular health risk.

mono-unsaturated fats A group of oils made up of triglycerides rich in mono-unsaturated fatty acids.

mono-unsaturated fatty acids Fatty acids in which the carbon chain contains one double bond.

MUFA Mono-unsaturated fatty acid.

myocardial infarction Death of a part of the heart muscle.

myocardium The heart muscle.

niacin One of the B group of vitamins. In mega-doses (over 1 gram a day) it has been shown to have a cholesterol-lowering effect. It has a number of side effects at these doses, and should only be taken under medical supervision.

nicotinic acid Niacin.

nicotinic acid derivatives Group of drugs based on nicotinic acid.

noradrenline This can be released along with adrenaline in times of danger and stress. It acts to constrict blood vessels.

oat bran A rich source of soluble fibre.

obesity Being severely overweight.

oils A subgroup of the lipids. Oils are similar to the fats, except that they are liquid at room temperature.

omega-3 fatty acids A group of polyunsaturated fatty acids in which the first double bond is between the third and fourth carbon atoms. This group of lipids includes EPA.

opportunistic screening A policy whereby the general public is checked for a particular health risk as and when the opportunity arises.

phospholipids A group of lipids which have phosphorus, and usually nitrogen, associated with them. Within the lipoprotein structures they act as wetting agents.

platelets Small particles in the blood that are involved in the clotting process. Because of this they are involved in atherosclerotic deposits.

polyunsaturated fats Fats and oils which contain poly-unsaturated fatty acids.

polyunsaturated fatty acids Fatty acids in which the carbon chain contains more than one double bond.

primary When referring to a symptom or a health problem, it indicates that the disease and the symptom are one and the same.

probucol A prescription drug causing loss of bile salts in the faeces, a lowering of LDL and a slight lowering of HDL.

protein Consist largely of carbon, hydrogen and nitrogen. They are made up of many amino acids.

PUFA Polyunsaturated fatty acid.

saturated fats Fats and oils which contain mainly saturated fatty acids.

saturated fatty acids Fatty acids in which the carbon chain contains no double bonds.

screening Checking the general population, or sections of it, for a health problem.

secondary When referring to a symptom or a health problem, it indicates that the symptom is caused by a separate disease, or is the side effect of a drug or of the lifestyle.

selective screening A policy by which certain sections of the general public are checked for a particular health problem.

simple carbohydrates Short-chain carbohydrates built up from simple sugars and little else.

soluble fibre Dietary fibre that can absorb water and other compounds in the gut. Found mainly in the pulses and fruit, and to lesser extent in cereal foods.

sterols A group of lipids that includes cholesterol and many hormones.

stroke Often called a CVA of cerebrovascular accident, it is an interruption to the blood supply to the
brain, invariably caused by atheroclerosis.

sugars The basic building blocks of carbohydrates;
carbohydrates are broken down into sugars by the
process of digestion.

systole The pumping phase of the heart's cycle.

systolic pressure Blood pressure during systole. It is
greater than the diastolic pressure.

triglyceride A fat or oil consisting of a glycerol backbone to which are attached three fatty acids.

veins Blood vessels bringing blood from the peripheral
tissues back to the heart.

very low density lipoprotein An early stage in the
production of cholesterol-rich low density lipoprotein.

VLDL Very low density lipoprotein.

western diet General term for a diet that is high in
processed foods, rich in fats, particularly rich in
saturated fats, and low in dietary fibre and complex
carbohydrates.

xanthelasmas Blobs rich in cholesterol that develop
around the eye or eyelid in those who have raised
cholesterol levels.

xanthomas Cholesterol deposits found on the ends of
tendons, especially the Achilles tendon, or under the
skin on the elbows or palms in those with high
cholesterol levels.

Further reading

The first two books are academically orientated, and might prove a little heavy going. However, for those who have the scientific or medical background they make very interesting reading:

Handbook of Coronary Heart Disease Prevention, edited by Barry Lewis, Gerd Assman, Mario Mancini and Yechezkiel Stein, Current Medical Literature, London, 1989.
Lipids and Heart Disease: A Practical Approach, by Madeleine Ball and Jim Mann, Oxford University Press, Oxford, 1988.

Now, a book that is aimed at the general public:

A Healthy Heart For Life, by Dr Caroline Shreeve, Thorsons, London, 1988.

And finally, a range of cookbooks designed to help you produce meals that are part of a cholesterol lowering programme. The first is a companion volume to this book:

The FHA Low-Fat Diet Book, by David Symes and Annette Zakary, Optima, London, 1991.

Dr Anderson's HCF Diet, by Dr James Anderson, Optima, London, 1984.

The Healthy Heart Diet Book, by Roberta Longstaff and Dr Jim Mann, Optima, London, 1986.

The Oat Cookbook, by Mary Cadogan and Shirley Bond, Optima, London, 1987.

Useful addresses

Family Heart Association
7 High Street
Kidlington OX5 2DH
Tel 0865 370292 Fax 0865 370295

British Heart Foundation
14 Fitzhardinge Street
London W1H 4DH

Chest, Heart and Stroke Association
Tavistock House North
Tavistock Square
London WC1H 9JE

Chest, Heart and Stroke Association, Scottish Branch
65 North Castle Street
Edinburgh EH2 3LT

Northern Ireland Chest, Heart and Stroke Association
21 Dublin Road
Belfast BT2 7FJ

AUSTRALIA
National Heart Foundation of Australia
National Office
PO Box 2
WODEN ACT 2606

IRELAND
Irish Heart Foundation
4 Clyde Road
Ballsbridge
Dublin 4

UNITED STATES
American Heart Association
National Center
7320 Greenville Avenue
Dallas
Texas 75231

National Cholesterol Education Program
National Heart, Lung and Blood Institute
National Institutes of Health
C-200
Bethesda
Maryland 20892

The Family Heart Association

The Family Heart Association (FHA) was originally founded in 1982 by two young mothers who had inherited familial hypercholesterolaemia (FH). This condition causes dangerously high levels of cholesterol in the blood and greatly increases the chances of having a heart attack at a young age. Far too few people were aware of the existence of FH and the devastating consequences it can have, so the FHA worked:

* To inform and support those affected by FH and other inherited hyperlipidaemias.
* To increase awareness of inherited hyperlipidaemias amongst the medical profession and the public.
* To encourage and support research into the causes and treatment of these conditions.

The FHA encourages those with a family history of heart attacks to ask their GPs for a full coronary heart disease risk assessment, including a blood cholesterol test, blood pressure, weight, diet, lifestyle, family history of coronary heart disease, personal medical history and medical examination. If the blood cholesterol level is found to be raised, or if other risk factors

193

are detected, the most important initial treatment is to adopt a healthy diet, with foods low in saturated (animal) fats. To this end the FHA can supply dietary guidance and other helpful information.

For more details about the FHA, its publications and its support services, contact:

Family Heart Association
7 High Street
Kidlington OX5 2DH
Tel 0865 370292 Fax 0865 370295

Index

Page numbers in *italic* refer to pages including illustrations